UNBROKEN SERVICE
THE HISTORY OF LLOYD'S PATRIOTIC FUND
1803–2003

Charles Messenger

UNBROKEN SERVICE
THE HISTORY OF LLOYD'S PATRIOTIC FUND 1803–2003

Copyright © 2003 Lloyd's Patriotic Fund
First published in the UK in 2003 by
MDA Communications, Southbank House,
Black Prince Road, London SE1 7SJ
Telephone 020 7463 2020
Facsimile 020 7463 2008
info@mdacomms.com

ISBN 0-9542481-1-2

Printed in the UK at Redgate Press

Cover: William Lionel Wyllie's Panorama of the Battle of Trafalgar.
© ROYAL NAVAL MUSEUM

Lloyd's Patriotic Fund
1 Lime Street
London
EC3M 7HA
Tel: +44 (0) 20 7327 5925
Fax: +44 (0) 20 7327 6368
Email: lloyds-external-enquiries@lloyds.com

CONTENTS

FOREWORD

Admiral Sir Alan West KCB DSC
Chief of the Naval Staff
and First Sea Lord

Lloyd's close connection with the Royal Navy stretches back to well into the 18th century, when it was bound by their mutual interest in protecting mercantile trade in time of war. In the 1780s Lloyd's began to provide charitable support to the Navy through a series of subscriptions raised to help those wounded in the service of their country and the dependants of sailors who had perished. It was through these, and the presentations of plate made by Lloyd's to him for his victories, that Horatio Nelson forged a relationship with John Julius Angerstein of Lloyd's and became an enthusiastic supporter of the Patriotic Fund and all that it stood for. Given this background, it is a distinct honour for me, as the professional head of today's Royal Navy, to be invited to write a Foreword to Lloyd's Patriotic Fund's

bicentennial history. In its early years the Patriotic Fund not only gave much help to sailors, soldiers and their families who had suffered during the long war against Napoleon Buonaparte, but also rewarded individuals for meritorious and gallant conduct in action against Britain's enemies. Most notable were the Patriotic Fund swords, which were worn with great pride by those awarded them. But, with ever increasing casualties, especially as a result of the Peninsular War, it was understandable and right that Lloyd's should cease this practice and allow this fund to devote its resources entirely to the relief of suffering.

Since then, many thousands of sailors, soldiers and, more recently, airmen, and their loved ones who have fallen on hard times as a result of death, wounds and

sickness have been helped by Lloyd's Patriotic Fund. It has enabled lives to be rebuilt and given children opportunities that would otherwise have been denied to them. While the Fund is now but one of a number of active Service charities, Britain's Armed Forces recognise it as the longest serving and remain deeply grateful for its invaluable work. Long may Lloyd's Patriotic Fund continue to provide the help that it does.

Alan West

William Lionel Wyllie's Panorama of the Battle of Trafalgar. It depicts the situation at 2pm, when the battle was some two hours old. HMS Victory is in the centre with shell splashes on her port side. *Painting: © ROYAL NAVAL MUSEUM*

PREFACE

Lord Peter Levene of Portsoken KBE
The Chairman of Lloyd's

Lloyd's has always been very proud of the work of its Patriotic Fund and its unbroken service to the welfare of Britain's Armed Forces. It is therefore fitting that Lloyd's Patriotic Fund's story should be marked by a new History in this its bicentennial year. It was founded at a time when Britain stood alone and, not for the first or the last time, faced the very real threat of invasion. Since that time, it has provided charitable support to Britain's servicemen and women, and their dependants, who have suffered as a result of numerous conflicts in which this country has been engaged.

The Trustees of Lloyd's Patriotic Fund have always given their services and time voluntarily and have been pleased to do so. Indeed, they personify the spirit of the Lloyd's community, which has long been conscious of the need to help others. Today this is reflected in Lloyd's Charities Trust, which is involved in a wide range of charitable endeavours. Tribute, too, must be paid to those who have served as Secretary to Lloyd's Patriotic Fund.

On their shoulders has rested the day-to-day administration of the Fund, a task which they have always carried out with great dedication. In its early years, Lloyd's Patriotic Fund was a national institution because it accurately reflected the mood of the Country and was unique. Its example was followed in time by others, notably the Royal Patriotic Fund established at the beginning of the Crimean War and the National Relief Fund of 1914-18, besides a plethora of other Service charities. These days the public profile of Lloyd's Patriotic Fund may not be what it once was, but the work it does is just as important and reflects Lloyd's continuing admiration for Britain's Armed Forces.

Levene of Portsoken.

DONORS

The Trustees of the Lloyd's Patriotic Fund wish to thank the following major donors whose generosity has made the production of this book possible.

AUTHOR'S INTRODUCTION AND ACKNOWLEDGEMENTS

by Charles Messenger

I first became aware of Lloyd's Patriotic Fund as a boy. An avid reader of C S Forester, I noted that his hero Horatio Hornblower was awarded a Patriotic Fund sword to the value of fifty guineas [sic] and was clearly deeply honoured by this recognition of his exploits in the Mediterranean while commanding the sloop HMS *Atropos*. Unfortunately, nowhere in his Hornblower books does Forester make mention of the Patriotic Fund's main work of the time – the provision of financial assistance to the wounded and the families of those who had fallen in action. It was to be many years before I became aware of this and it was only when I came to do my research for this History that I began to realise the extent of the support that Lloyd's Patriotic Fund has given to the Armed Forces over the past two hundred years and, perhaps even more important, the inspiration that it provided for other Service charities. Indeed, without Lloyd's initiative in establishing the Fund, it is questionable whether today's Armed Forces would have the benefit of the significant number of charities dedicated to them.

It has therefore been a pleasure to write this book, but I could not have done it without the help of others. First and foremost, I am most grateful to Charles Skey, Chairman of Lloyd's Patriotic Fund, for his support and encouragement. Indeed, it was he and his committee who conceived the idea of a new history. Mrs Linda Harper, Secretary to the Fund, was most helpful in making introductions and administering the project on behalf of the Fund. Thanks, too, go to her secretary Janis Hunt. Richard Keene also has my gratitude. He provided essential books from the Lloyd's Library and was tireless in his efforts to produce illustrations for the book. His knowledge of the history of Lloyd's was also invaluable. Charles Skey,

Clive de Rougemont, Linda Harper and Richard Keene read the manuscript in draft and I much appreciate their comments. Much of my primary research was carried out at the Guildhall Library and I would like to thank the staff of the Manuscripts Department for their unfailing courtesy and helpfulness.

Finding suitable illustrations involved a number of people. Apart from the staffs of the galleries, museums, and picture libraries which are credited in the book, I would like to thank the following individuals for their efforts on my behalf – Neil Acheson-Gray, Patrick Dealtry (The Corps of Commissionaires), Mrs Fiona Duncan and Mrs Louise Tarry (Royal School, Haslemere), Richard Howells, Richard Hulley (Royal High School, Bath), Mrs Dawn Lambert, and Don Topley (Royal Hospital School, Holbrook). Finally, I deeply appreciate the work of MDA Publishing in turning the raw material into a book. In particular, my thanks go to the Managing Director, Colonel Michael Dewar, for inviting me to write the History and for steering it through, James Dewar, Lisa Crowe and James Greenfield who designed it, and, last but not least, Laura Gibbons, the production manager, whose patience and dedication to the project knew no bounds.

London, March 2003

Chapter One
IN THE BEGINNING

The Napoleonic Wars were a titanic struggle that, like so many of Britain's major conflicts, especially the two World Wars, began badly, with only a few shafts of light to brighten the gloom. Lasting for well over 20 years, they called for the very best in the British character, especially doggedness and self-belief. It was at the very darkest period of the long war against France that Lloyd's Patriotic Fund was conceived and born. Those who created it reflected this bulldog spirit and the enthusiasm with which it was supported demonstrated that the Patriotic Fund's founders had their fingers on the nation's pulse.

Lloyd's itself could be said to have come of age during the early years of the 19th century. Yet its origins lay in one of the many coffee houses that began to spring up in London in the late 17th and early 18th centuries. They became the centres for gathering news and for the transaction of business. Lloyd's Coffee House itself is first mentioned in the *London Gazette* in February 1689, although the issue was actually dated 1688 because up until 1752, when Britain changed from the Julian to the Gregorian Calendar, the new year began on 26 March. The coffee house itself belonged to Edward Lloyd and was situated in Tower Street, moving to Lombard Street three years later.

In 1696, Lloyd started a newspaper with the prime objective of providing news on shipping, since his establishment had begun to become a meeting place for those involved in mercantile trade, especially insurers. *Lloyd's News* was published three times a week. It covered war news, for

England was engaged at the time in the War of the Grand Alliance against France, as well as domestic items and shipping intelligence from the ports. Lloyd, however, ceased publication within a year, apparently after a complaint from the Quakers over a false report in his newspaper that they had petitioned the House of Lords to relieve them of all public offices.

Lloyd himself died in 1712, but by this time his coffee house had become well known in the City. Richard Steele wrote in *Tatler*, which he had founded in 1709, that it had a pulpit, from which auctions were conducted, and that 'it was the custom on the first coming in of news, to order a youth, who officiates as the 'kidney' of the coffee house, to get into the pulpit, and read every paper with a loud distinct voice, while the whole audience are sipping their respective liquors'. But in spite of Lloyd's death, his coffee house lived on under the same name.

The period 1720–39 was a time of particular prosperity for the country under Prime Minister Robert Walpole, who was determined not to embroil Britain in another continental war. Foreign trade increased significantly, resulting in more ship insurance and a sharp rise in the number of the Underwriters, who were beginning to base themselves at Lloyd's. One particular inducement was the setting up of a new publication, *Lloyd's List*, which quickly became the best source of shipping intelligence in the country. Indeed, when Britain did find herself at war again, this time against Spain because of trade rivalries

in the Caribbean, it was *Lloyd's List* that first brought Walpole the news of Admiral Vernon's capture of Portobello on the Spanish Main in 1739.

The Prime Minister was unable to contain the war from becoming engulfed by a wider conflict, which was brought about by rival contenders for the throne of the Hapsburg Empire. By 1742, Britain had been drawn into the War of the Austrian Succession. For the Underwriters at Lloyd's it was an anxious time. Shipping losses rose, even though the Royal Navy did its best to organise convoys. Often, merchant skippers, knowing that their vessels were insured, would break convoy to reach port early so that their cargoes could be placed on the market before those of their competitors. The upshot was that shipping losses increased from 107 in 1741 to more than 450 during 1747, the penultimate year of the war, and Lloyd's Underwriters were forced to dig deep into their pockets.

Apart from the Walpole period, 18th-century Britain was dominated by war. Within ten years of the Treaty of Aix La Chapelle, which brought the War of the Austrian Succession to an end, the Seven Years War broke out. Again, France was the principal enemy. Then, trouble arose with the colonists in America, whose main objections were that they were being taxed from Westminster without having any representation there and that they believed that the British were imposing unfair trading terms on them. Relations grew so bad that open war broke out in 1776. Eventually, it drew in both the French and the Spanish on the side of the colonists. For British arms on land, the war eventually turned out as a disaster and the colonists gained their independence. At sea there was, however, one notable triumph, when Admiral Rodney decisively defeated the French fleet off the Islands of the Saints in the Caribbean in April 1782 and regained Britain's dominant position at sea. But this came too late for some of the Underwriters at Lloyd's.

Two years earlier, in August 1780, two British convoys, one bound for the West Indies and one for the East Indies, were caught with an inadequate escort prior to going their separate ways. Only eight out of the 63 merchantmen escaped ambush by the combined fleets of France and Spain, in part because the inadequate number of escort vessels had deserted them at the first sight of the enemy sails. The result was a monetary loss of £1,500,000, a huge sum in those times, and a number of Lloyd's Underwriters were made insolvent.

By this time, however, Lloyd's itself had adopted a more formal organisation. There had been no bars on anyone setting up as an Underwriter and the coffee house had begun to attract people who merely wanted to make a quick fortune. Matters came to a head in the 1760s when the end of the Seven Years War resulted in the collapse of the high wartime insurance rates on shipping, and these freebooters looked for other means to make money. They began to gamble on the lives of prominent men who were sick, on the likelihood of a new war with France and Spain, and other more frivolous ventures. This gave Lloyd's a bad name and the more reputable underwriters decided that enough was enough. In 1769 they broke away, setting up in new premises at 5 Pope's Head Alley, a street which still exists to this day. They called themselves the New Lloyd's Coffee House and began publishing their own *Lloyd's List*.

Two years later, 79 merchants, brokers and underwriters put their names to a document that marked the beginning of Lloyd's as we know it today. They agreed to subscribe £100 each to be placed in the Bank of England under the names of a committee elected by the subscribers. Also their new premises were not wholly satisfactory, being too cramped, and so a decision was made to find another base. Significantly, it was the subscribers and not the coffee-house proprietor who decided on the move, which took place in March 1774. The New Lloyd's was now situated over the northwest corner of the Royal Exchange and this was to be its home for the next 50 years and more.

By 1786, the Old Lloyd's was no more. The creation of its rival, with a committee made up of some of its most astute subscribers, even though for some years it contented itself with merely overseeing New Lloyd's accommodation, proved too powerful for the comparative anarchy that existed at the Lombard Street establishment.

The experience of the American War of Independence had confirmed Lloyd's realisation of how dependent it was on the Royal Navy for the protection of mercantile trade in time of war. The subscribers also began to recognise the sacrifices that British seamen made and how little help there was for those disabled by wounds and the dependants of those killed in action. True, under the patronage of Charles II and subsequent monarchs, the Royal Hospital for former soldiers at Chelsea, together with a similar institution in Ireland had been established by the early 18th century. Queen Mary, William III's consort, had also founded a similar home for the Navy at Greenwich.

They could, however, only take in a fraction of deserving ex-soldiers and seamen. Thanks to James II, the Army had also established a system of pensions, as well as gratuities for the wounded. Seamen, however, were generally not as well provided for, largely because the system was hopelessly inefficient. The seaman was not paid his wages in cash, but was issued with a 'ticket' on the decommissioning of his ship and this could only be cashed at the Navy Pay Office in London. Because of the cost of travelling from his port of discharge, the seaman would often cash the ticket with unscrupulous traders, who would give him only a fraction of what it was worth. Attempting to arrange for money to be passed to his dependants was a nightmare.

The subscribers at Lloyd's became increasingly aware of this and in 1782 initiated a fund at the Royal Exchange for the sufferers from HMS *Royal George* which sank at her moorings on 29 August with a large loss of life. They succeeded in raising nearly £7,000. There was, however, one Service charity that had now come into existence, the United Society for the Relief of Widows and Children of Seamen, Soldiers and Marines and Militiamen. Among other agencies, Lloyd's Coffee House acted as a collecting point for donations. But the help that the United Society could give was limited and it was about to become hopelessly overstretched.

The growing violence of the 1789 French Revolution soon made the other monarchs of Europe fear for their thrones. In February 1792, Austria and Prussia formed an alliance and were joined by the Kingdom of Sicily. They began to mass troops on the French borders and in April this led to the French National Assembly declaring war. For the time being, while the French, fired with revolutionary zeal, repulsed the allied invasions and drove them back, Britain remained on the sidelines. But when the revolutionaries guillotined Louis XVI in January 1793, the government felt that it

LLOYD'S COFFEE HOUSE

must take action and expelled the French Ambassador to London. The French immediately retaliated by declaring war on Britain, Spain and the Netherlands. They also occupied Belgium. The British sent a ground force to cooperate with the allies in the Low Countries. After early successes, which almost brought France to collapse, the Allies were driven back and the British troops returned to Britain, giving rise to the nursery rhyme 'The Grand Old Duke of York' who 'had ten thousand men' and 'marched them up to the top of the hill and marched them down again.' It was, however, the war at sea that most concerned the Lloyd's subscribers. There was an early success when the British Mediterranean Fleet, assisted by a Spanish squadron, seized the naval arsenal at Toulon, as well as many French ships. But, thanks largely to the efforts of a youthful artillery colonel called Napoleon Buonaparte, the French forced the allies to withdraw.

The years 1794–96 were marked by a number of British amphibious expeditions to support royalist uprisings in France. All were abortive. There was, however, one bright gleam at sea. In April 1794, a large French convoy of grain ships set out across the Atlantic from the United States. To protect it from the British Channel Fleet under Admiral Lord Richard Howe, the French fleet at Brest put to sea. Between 29 May and 1 June the two fleets fought a running battle 400 miles off Ushant. Howe captured six French ships and sank a seventh, forcing his opponent to withdraw to port. The convoy itself got through unscathed, but in Britain the Glorious First of June was celebrated as a great victory.

At Lloyd's a meeting of subscribers and others 'with liberality which will ever distinguish that respectable body of men, in less than one hour subscribed a thousand guineas'. They formed a committee and asked the public to donate

to the fund, even persuading the dramatist Richard Brinsley Sheridan to lay on a special performance starring Mrs Siddons and Mrs Jordan at his Drury Lane theatre, which raised £1,300. In all, the fund collected over £21,000 for the relief of Howe's crews and their dependants. This was much appreciated by the Admiralty, to whom Lloyd's was proving valuable in other ways as well.

Lloyd's intelligence was often more accurate and timely than the Navy's. Thus, it was able to report the capture of a British vessel by a French privateer off Lowestoft in 1794 and even the number of prizes taken by the latter since it set sail from Dunkirk before the Admiralty even knew about it. In return, Lloyd's received confidential details of the plans for the assembly and sailing of convoys and its comments on them were listened to with respect. In particular, the Admiralty heeded Lloyd's complaint that one warship was insufficient protection for a convoy.

Likewise, Lloyd's received complaints from escort commanders on merchantmen who broke away from convoys or otherwise disobeyed orders. Lloyd's then made a judgement which they passed on to the Admiralty.

Apart from at sea, the war continued to go badly for the allies. In 1795, the French overran the Netherlands, renaming it the Batavian Republic. Prussia, financially exhausted by the war, made peace with France and was followed by most of the German states and Spain, which ceded San Domingo in the West Indies. Spain then allied herself to France. The Austrians battled on, both in Germany and northern Italy, but after their country was invaded in 1797 they were forced to sue for peace, leaving Britain on her own.

At sea, the war was characterised by attacks on trade, with the frigates of both sides enjoying much success. For the British

crews this meant prize money, which could make fortunes for the admirals and captains involved and sometimes the equivalent of more than a year's pay for the ordinary seaman. In the City, a committee was established 'for encouraging the capture of French Privateers'. This awarded swords, plates and gratuities to successful crews and in one case Lloyd's underwriters also presented a piece of plate to Vice Admiral Kingsmill for the 'gallant defence of our trade on the Irish station'.

The Royal Navy also blockaded the port of Brest, but, once the Spanish became allied with the French, it was forced to abandon the blockade of Toulon and indeed withdraw the Mediterranean Fleet. The blockade of Brest was also not tight enough and in December 1796 a French force was able set sail from the port with the intention of invading Ireland. Only bad weather prevented it from landing. February 1797 brought better news.

The blowing up of the French flagship Orient marked the climax of the Battle of the Nile. *Painting: © NATIONAL MARITIME MUSEUM, London*

Admiral Sir John Jervis intercepted a Spanish fleet near Cape St Vincent on the Portuguese coast. The Spaniards were *en route* to join the French at Brest for an invasion of England and, although outnumbered by almost two to one, Jervis succeeded in scattering them, capturing four of their ships and forcing the remainder to seek refuge in Cadiz. Commodore Horatio Nelson, who was commanding HMS *Captain*, seized two of the prizes. Lloyd's marked the victory by raising another subscription, which totalled £2,615, for the dependants of the 73 men killed and to assist the 273 men who had been wounded in the action.

Two months after the victory at Cape St Vincent, the Royal Navy was rocked by a mutiny. It started at Spithead and spread rapidly. The mutineers were demanding better conditions on board and maintained their stance for several weeks, putting several ships out of commission. The mutinies were put down and in October 1797 the Navy showed that its effectiveness had been restored when Admiral Duncan virtually destroyed a Dutch fleet at Camperdown in the North Sea. The relief in the City and the nation as a whole was shown by another Lloyd's subscription, which raised the impressive total of £52,609 for those who were casualties in the battle. This enabled no less than 5,900 widows and children to be helped from the fund, as well as numerous wounded.

The year 1798 saw the Royal Navy re-enter the Mediterranean. The decision resulted from intelligence that Napoleon Buonaparte, who was rapidly becoming the leading light in France, was intending to invade Egypt. His reason for doing this was to pose such a threat to India that the British would be forced to sue for peace. Nelson was despatched with a small fleet, but was unable to locate the French invasion force, which duly landed and decisively defeated the Egyptians at the Battle of the Pyramids. But Nelson did discover the French fleet anchored close to the shore in Aboukir Bay.

On 1 August he led part of his own fleet between the French ships and the shore, while the other part attacked from seaward. Only two out of the thirteen French ships escaped destruction and got away. Once more there were celebrations in Britain and Nelson became a national hero overnight. Another subscription was opened at Lloyd's, raising the sum of £38,436.

John Julius Angerstein (of whom more later), the Chairman of Lloyd's Nile Committee, wrote to Nelson on 10 October asking him to furnish lists of killed and wounded in the action, which the Admiral consented to do. The Committee also voted Nelson a collection of plate to the value of £500, commissioning Rundell & Bridge 'Jewellers and Goldsmiths to Their Majesties' to make it. This appears to have taken a long time, since it was not ready until late 1800 and Nelson himself did not receive it until the following year, although he certainly visited Lloyd's in person on 15 November 1800. Lloyd's also voted £1,000 from its collective funds towards the Voluntary Subscription for National Defence, which was set up in 1798 to enhance the government's war chest.

In 1798 there were better prospects for Britain than in recent years, since in December Emperor Paul of Russia formed the second coalition of allies against France. Its members were Russia, Britain, Austria, Portugal, Naples, the Vatican and the Ottoman Empire. However, it eventually proved, alas, no more successful than the previous coalition. True, largely Russian forces did drive the French out of northern Italy during 1799, but efforts to expel them from Switzerland failed. An Anglo-Russian attempt to overrun the Netherlands also failed, although the British managed to seize the Dutch fleet. The campaigns of 1800 saw Napoleon drive an Austrian army out of Switzerland and then force its surrender after the decisive Battle of Marengo, while another French army advanced through Germany, defeating the remaining Austrian

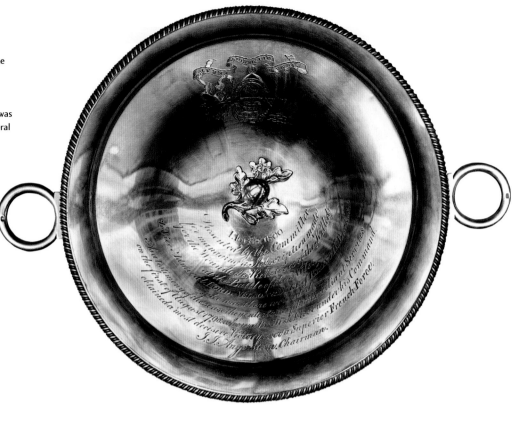

Soup Tureen inscribed: 'Lloyd's Coffee House, A Tribute of Gratitude and respect from his Country to the Memory of Captain John Harvey of His Majesty's Ship, The Brunswick, who gloriously fell in the Important Action of the 1st of June 1794 when the French Fleet was defeated by the British Fleet under Command of Admiral Earl Howe, John Julius Angerstein Chairman.'
Photograph: © LLOYD'S

forces at Hohenlinden in December. This forced the Austrians to make peace. Only in Egypt did the allies enjoy success on land. British forces landed there in March 1801, defeated the French forces, but allowed them free passage back to France.

Following Austria's second exit from the war, Russia too withdrew to the sidelines and the British focus now switched to the Baltic. Russia, Prussia, Denmark and Sweden had formed the Neutral League. Buonaparte granted free passage without interference to its ships and the League demanded that Britain also respect their neutrality and not stop and search them. Realising that this would inevitably mean that the Neutral League would now trade with France, the British Government acted quickly. It despatched a powerful naval squadron under Sir Hyde Parker, with Nelson as his second-in-command, to the Baltic.

The intention was to disarm Denmark's sizeable fleet before it could combine with the Swedes and Russians and bar the Baltic to British shipping. Nelson realised the need for speed, even if his elderly superior was more hesitant. Arriving off Copenhagen, an ultimatum was sent to the Danes, who rejected it. Parker was in favour of waiting, but Nelson was not. On 2 April 1801, he led his squadron against the Danish fleet. In the subsequent bombardment, the Danes used their floating batteries to good effect, causing some 200 casualties aboard HMS Monarch alone. Three of Nelson's ships were grounded and Parker ordered him to break off the engagement. Nelson refused to be deterred, making his famous 'I do not see the signal' comment, as he put his telescope to his blind eye. After five hours of pounding the Danes had had enough. The British squadron then moved to threaten the Russian ships at Kronstadt, but the new Czar Alexander had absorbed the message of Copenhagen. The Neutral League acknowledged the British right to stop and search its ships and the Baltic remained open for British trade.

Once more there was rejoicing in Britain, with Nelson's standing now even higher in the public's estimation. A Lloyd's subscription raised £15,500 and Angerstein sent another letter to Nelson requesting a casualty return. In his reply, Nelson wrote: 'I feel – and am certain every Officer and man in the Fleet does the same – much indebted to the Gentlemen of the Committee for the attention they pay, and trouble they experience, on this occasion.' He also said that he hoped to visit Lloyd's soon to thank them all personally. In addition, the Copenhagen Committee voted the Admiral another £500 worth of plate, but this time Nelson was allowed to select his own, using his agent, Alexander Davison, to give the necessary instructions to Rundell & Bridge. The inscription on it read as follows:

Presented by the Committee appointed to manage the Subscription raised for the benefit of the Wounded and the Relatives of those who were Killed in the glorious Victory obtained off Copenhagen on the 2 of April 1801,

To Vice Admiral Lord Nelson, K.B., Duke of Bronte, &c, &c, &c.
In testimony of the high sense entertained of his meritorious exertions in the defence of his Country, which at the peril and danger of his life, he so nobly sustained previous to the Engagement, and as a token of his brilliant and gallant Conduct during the whole of that ever memorable Action.

John Julius Angerstein, Chairman, Lloyd's Coffee House

By this time, however, Britain was beginning to suffer from war weariness.

Vegetable dish from the Nile Service presented by Lloyd's to Nelson after his victory off the Egyptian coast.
Photograph: © LLOYD'S

One indication of this was the low amounts raised by Lloyd's in two subscriptions subsequent to Copenhagen. In August 1801, Nelson attempted to capture barges gathered at Boulogne for a possible invasion of England. The French batteries proved too powerful and he was forced to withdraw. Lloyd's raised a mere £640. Likewise, after Sir James Saumarez had the best of an action against a more powerful Franco-Spanish fleet off Algerciras the previous month, a fund for the casualties and their dependants collected just £668. The truth of the matter was that the war had reached stalemate. Britain might dominate the seas, but she lacked the means to bring direct influence to bear on events in continental Europe. There was also recognition that France, now under Napoleon Buonaparte, was a very different place to the turbulent nation that it had been when Britain had gone to war in 1793. France might dominate Europe, but the country was stable and the revolutionary bacillus, which had threatened to reduce the whole of Europe to a state of anarchy, was dead.

Consequently, the government opened negotiations for peace. Buonaparte, too, seemed willing to bring the conflict to an end and on 1 October 1801 a Preliminary Treaty was signed. This was formalised by the Treaty of Amiens the following March and Europe was once more at peace. It would not last long. Napoleon, who had been made First Consul for life in August 1802 and had dropped Buonaparte from his name, was soon scheming to regain control of Egypt and drive the British out of India. Relations between Britain and France deteriorated. Eventually, on 16 May 1803, Britain declared war and the Royal Navy re-imposed its blockade of French ports.

A month after the renewal of hostilities, the Lloyd's Committee received a petition signed by 33 subscribers. They asked for a special general meeting to be convened to consider their proposal that a Patriotic Fund be established on a permanent basis to provide relief for those wounded and the dependants of those killed in the defence of the country. This, they believed, would be considerably more beneficial than raising subscriptions for particular battles and merely assisting the victims of these. The Committee readily acceded to their request and on 20 July 1803 a number of subscribers to Lloyd's Coffee House met under the chairmanship of Mr Brooke Watson.

Watson was one the great characters of Lloyd's of the day. Born in 1735 at Plymouth, he was orphaned at an early age and went to sea at 14, only to lose his leg to a shark off Havana, an incident which was immortalised in a painting by the American-born artist John Singleton Copley (1737–1815) which today hangs in the Smithsonian Museum, Washington DC. Watson served as a commissary during the Seven Years War, including supplying food and stores to General James Wolfe's troops in Canada. He then became a merchant and joined Lloyd's, rising to become the first Chairman of the Committee formed in 1772. Towards the end of the American War of Independence he served as Commissary-General in Canada and in 1784 was elected Member of Parliament for the City of London. In 1793 he gave up his seat and was made Commissary-General to the British Forces in Flanders during the 1793–95 campaign. On his return, and a measure of the esteem in which he was held, Watson became Lord Mayor of London. Then, in March 1798, he was made Commissary-General to the forces in Great Britain. He was also a Director of the Bank of England.

The meeting itself passed a number of resolutions and the first of these encapsulated the mood of those who were present:

That in a conjuncture, when the vital Interest of our Country, when the peculiar Blessings, which, under our beloved Sovereign and happy Constitution, endear our Social State, are involved in the issue of the present Conflict when we are menaced by an Enemy whose Haughty Presumption is grounded only on the present unfortunate Position of the Continental Powers, and when we see to be placed for the moment, as the last Barrier against the total Subjugation of Europe by the Overbearing Influence of France It behoves us to meet our Situation as Men – as Freemen – but above all as Britons. On this alone, with the divine Aid, depends our Exemption from the Yoke of Gallic Despotism – on this alone depends, under the same Protecting Power, whether the Empire shall remain what it has for ages been, the strenuous supporter of religion and morals, the assertor of its own, and the guardian of the liberties of mankind, the nurse of industry, the protector of the arts and sciences, the example and admiration of the world – or whether it shall become the obsequious tributary, an enslaved, a plundered, and degraded department of a foreign nation.

The subscribers went on to agree that 'it behoves us to hold out every encouragement to our fellow-subjects, who may be in any way instrumental in repelling or annoying our implacable foe: and to prove to them that we are ready to drain both our purses and our veins in the greater cause which imperiously calls us to unite the duties of loyalty and patriotism, with the strongest efforts of zealous exertions'. To this end, it was resolved to establish 'a suitable Fund for their comfort and relief – for the purpose of assuaging the anguish of their wounds, or palliating in some degree the more weighty misfortune of the loss of limbs – of alleviating the distresses of the widow and orphan – of smoothing the brow of sorrow for the fall of dearest relations – and of granting pecuniary rewards, or honourable badges of distinction, for successful exertions of valour or merit'.

Thus were the aims of the Patriotic Fund laid down, to provide charitable support on the one hand and to reward on the other. As to how the monies to support the Fund should be raised, the meeting agreed that it should look not only to the institutions and the Great and the Good, but also 'to our fellow-subjects of every class and denomination'. No donation, however small, would be turned down. To set the fund-raising going, the subscribers voted a donation of £20,000 in 3-per-cent Consolidated Stock (Consols). The meeting agreed to meet in a week's time for the purpose of appointing a committee 'for the receipt and management of the Subscriptions, and other purposes expressed in these Resolutions'. The minutes of the meeting were also to be published in the press.

The accuracy that those who set up the Patriotic Fund had displayed in gauging the mood of the country was amply demonstrated at their next meeting, on 29 July, when it was announced that more than £74,200 had already been subscribed. The Bank of England and the Honourable East India Company each gave £10,000, the City of London £2500, and the three principal insurance companies (Sun Fire Office, Royal Exchange Assurance, and London Assurance) £2,000 each. A number of Lloyd's subscribers personally donated the sum of £1,000 each.

The meeting elected a committee initially numbering 50 persons and it was agreed that nine members would represent a quorum. In subsequent meetings, a further 22 names were added to the committee. They included Jacob Bosanquet, Chairman of the Honourable East India Company, and his deputy, as well as the Governor of the Bank of England and the prime wardens of

Wine coolers, with Nelson's Coat of Arms prominently displayed, from Lloyd's Copenhagen Service. *Photograph: © LLOYD'S*

a number of livery companies. To start with, the Fund did not have its own office, but rented the Lloyd's Committee Room between the hours of 11am and 3pm for the sum of £50 per annum. The committee itself usually met weekly in the Merchant Seamen's Office.

By the time that the committee had met for the third time, the Patriotic Fund stood very close to £100,000. Money was now flowing in from the provinces, where local Fund committees were established in major cities. Thus, the Dublin Patriotic Fund initially subscribed £6,000, and subsequent donations boosted its share to nearly £29,000. The people of Durham raised some £4,400 but, in his covering letter, the Bishop of Durham, who personally subscribed an additional £1,000, proposed that the money raised should be used locally rather than go into the central fund. In its reply, the committee stated that it considered this a less efficient way of operating the Patriotic Fund and that it would be more open to fraud. It did, however, assure the Bishop that 'distant places' would be covered by the Fund. Mr George Coleman of the Theatre Royal, Haymarket offered to

contribute all receipts from one of the performances. The manager and the theatre at Grantham offered likewise, and sent a sum of £19 16s 4d. The Reverend Charles McCarthy offered his church in Spitalfields for a service in which he would preach a sermon extolling the virtues of the Fund, again an offer gratefully accepted by the committee.

Ships and regiments also subscribed. The officers and crew of HMS *Pickle* each gave a month's pay, apart from one man, whose reasons for declining were not revealed. Two sergeant-majors of His Majesty's Egyptian Brigade, commanded by Major General Finch, informed the committee that they had collected the sum of £111 5s 7d, with sergeants donating two days' pay and junior ranks one day. Whole families contributed. The 12 members of the Secretan family donated £122, together with a guinea from a friend and 12s 6d from their servants. Among more humble offerings were 4s from a Mr D P Hearnden, sent in four equal amounts, and 'the Mite of a half-pay Lieutenant, his wife, six sons and six daughters, all under age'. A farmer from Hunston in Suffolk, 17 labourers and a boy sent £2 17s 6d and a

shoemaker 2s 6d. There were donations from 'a few friends' from the Society of Free and Happy Britons and the Everlasting Society of Eccentrics. The Society of Friends, even though its Quaker beliefs would not countenance contributing to anything connected with war, was sufficiently moved to send 30 guineas for the provision of warm clothing for soldiers and sailors. Money too began to come in from the Colonies.

To ensure that the money was invested wisely, the committee appointed three trustees at its meeting held on 2 August 1803. The investments were to be made in their names and would be in Government Securities, principally Consols and Reduced.[1] The men appointed were among the leading lights of both Lloyd's and the City. Scotsman Thomson Bonar had joined Lloyd's in 1773 and had risen to become one of the most successful underwriters of the day. Sir Francis Baring, who was also elected Chairman of the Patriotic Fund in place of Brook Watson, who stood down at

[1]Consols represented the Consolidated Fund which was government monies held by the Bank of England, while Reduced was an investment in a sinking fund designed to reduce government debt.

the same meeting, was the founder of
Baring Brothers, which soon became one
of the leading City banks. He was also a
director of the East India Company and
became its Chairman in 1792. He was a
Member of Parliament and had written
three books on government and banking.
The fact that he was deaf from birth did
nothing to detract from his financial
acumen. Indeed, the *European Magazine* of
September 1810 described him as
'unquestionably the first merchant in
Europe, first in knowledge and talents,
and first in character and opulence'.

The third trustee was John Julius
Angerstein, a naturalised Briton, who
had been born in St Petersburg and
came to England in 1750, at the age of
15, under the patronage of a merchant
who specialised in trade with Russia.
After serving his apprenticeship as a clerk
in this man's counting house, Angerstein
was introduced to Lloyd's at the age of 21
and never looked back. He proved himself
to be a skilful underwriter and insurance
broker and gained wide respect. He was
also one of the main driving forces
behind Lloyd's efforts to modernise and
became its chairman in 1795. His easy
manner gained him a wide circle of
friends and his passionate interest in the
arts meant that it included such
luminaries as Samuel Johnson, the actor
David Garrick, and the painters Sir Joshua
Reynolds and Sir Thomas Lawrence. He
was also a philanthropist and the principal
initiator of the subscriptions raised by
Lloyd's to honour the principal naval
victories of the 1790s. William Pitt the
Younger valued his financial advice. With
these three men at the helm, the Patriotic
Fund would be in sure hands.

Yet, although the Fund was launched to
much popular acclaim, not all supported
it. One notable objector was William
Cobbett, the radical Tory journalist who
was editor of *Cobbett's Weekly Political
Register*. He had a loathing for the
merchant class and attacked the idea of
'a set of traders at Lloyd's' rewarding
officers and men for meritorious service,
when it was the right of the Crown alone
to bestow honours and awards. He
claimed that the Fund was not supported
by the aristocracy and landed gentry, even
though many were listed as subscribers to
it, and that the Patriotic Fund Committee
was driven by self-interest. Cobbett's
attacks almost certainly deterred some
from contributing to the Fund, but it had
its stalwart defenders, not least of which
was *The Times*. It launched a counter-blast,
calling Cobbett's barbs 'low, illiberal and
vulgar abuse' and declaring that 'the
Patriotic Fund will form in the eyes of
future ages, one of the brightest
ornaments of British glory'. The majority
of the British public took the Thunderer's
view and donations continued to flow in.
Now, with clashes at sea already taking
place, the Committee of the Patriotic
Fund was soon making its first awards.

Below: John Julius Angerstein (1735-1823) was one of the great figures of Lloyd's and the City of his day. He was the driving force behind a number of Lloyd's subscriptions prior to the establishment of the Patriotic Fund and an inspirational Chairman of both Lloyd's and the Patriotic Fund. *Painting: © LLOYD'S*

Right: Sir Francis Baring, founder of Baring's Bank and the Patriotic Fund's second Chairman. *Painting: By Charles Muss, after Sir Thomas Laurence (1806 –1807). Reproduced by Courtesy of the NATIONAL PORTRAIT GALLERY, London*

Chapter Two

ESTABLISHING THE GUIDELINES 1803-1804

At its meeting of 16 August 1803, less than a month after the Patriotic Fund had been established, the Committee decided on its first awards. Its main source of information was the *London Gazette*, which routinely published despatches sent to the Admiralty and War Office. After reading one of these, the Committee requested details of Lieutenant Temple, temporarily commanding the frigate *Loire*, concerning his recent highly successful operation to cut out the French gun brig *Ventroux* from under the noses of the coastal batteries on the Isle de Bas, which guards the port of Roscoff on the north coast of Brittany. They also asked for the names of the officers engaged and details of the wounded.

Within two weeks, Temple had replied and the Patriotic Fund rewarded Boatswain Mcguire and Sergeant John O'Reilly Royal Marines with the sum of £40 each, and four seamen £20 each. All, according to Temple, had been wounded and had distinguished themselves in the action. Three weeks later, the Committee received a letter from Major General Bowater of the Royal Marines claiming O'Reilly's reward on his behalf. The gallant sergeant was being treated at the Marine Barracks at Plymouth and the Committee replied to General Bowater's letter:

'They conceive the reward might not be paid until the Wounded Men are in a state of Convalescence, to prevent their injuring themselves; but if you will be so good as to see that the Money is properly applied for the Benefit of O'Reilly, the Committee request that you will please draw on Messrs Bennet & White of Lloyd's Coffee House for the sum.'

This remained the Fund's policy with regard to the wounded. They had no wish to see the recipient spend the money on drink and riotous living while his recovery still had some way to go. While most of these first awards were settled within a month, Seamen Job Parker and Samuel West had to wait until May 1804 before they received their money, presumably because their wounds were particularly severe. Indeed, from the beginning of 1804 the Committee insisted on a Certificate of Convalescence from a suitable public authority before agreeing to release the money.

Often, too, a man's wounds turned out to be more severe than originally thought. In these cases, the Committee frequently awarded additional sums of money. Thus, in August 1805 the Committee reconsidered the case of Corporal William Livins of the Royal Marines, who had been awarded £10 for a slight wound in the arm. They had in front of them a letter from Lieutenant General Barclay, commanding the Royal Marines at Chatham, in which he stated that Livins had now lost all use of the limb. The Committee therefore granted him an additional £30.

At the same meeting at which Lieutenant Temple's letter was considered, the Committee decided to approach artists for designs of 'marks of distinction for the gallant young officers who commanded the boats on that occasion'. Rewards of Fifty Guineas for the best Design, Thirty Guineas for the Second, Twenty Guineas for the Third, of a Medal, a Sword or a Vase, all or either of them' were offered. The results of this competition were announced in *The Times* of 2 December 1803.

Mr Edward Edwards and Mr John Shaw won the first prizes for the design of a medal and vase respectively. The Committee agreed that both would have the same inscriptions. Over the group of a warrior fighting a hydra the words, 'For our King, our Country, and our God' were to be inscribed, with 'Britons strike home' underneath. The reverse of each had the figure of Britannia presenting a laurel wreath, with the words, 'A grateful Country to her brave Defender' and 'Rule Britannia'.

No prize for the design of a sword was announced, but the contract for making them was awarded to Richard Teed of Lancaster Court, the Strand, London. There were to be three models – valued at £100, £50, and £30. The Committee also agreed that, on occasion, officers awarded swords could accept a sum of money *in lieu* to enable them to purchase swords of their own choice. In these cases the Committee would recommend a suitable inscription to commemorate the action that prompted the award.

The first to be awarded swords were the 'gallant young officers' of the *Loire*. Lieutenants Temple and Bowen were granted £50 swords and Midshipman Priest one of £30 in value. As was the practice adopted by the Committee,

Temple's and Priest's swords were sent to them, but Bowen's was presented to his father at a special ceremony held at Lloyd's on 19 June 1804.

Since Sir Francis Baring was detained in the House of Commons, Joseph Marryat was in the Chair. He, too, was one of Lloyd's leading figures of the day and the father of Captain Frederick Marryat RN, who became famous for his books about naval life and his, now classic, *Children of the New Forest*. Apart from many members of the Patriotic Fund Committee being present, Captain Austin Bissell was also due to receive a sword and Captain Watt was, like Bowen, representing his son, whose gallant conduct in cutting out a French armed lugger was to be similarly rewarded.

Joseph Marryat expressed the Committee's pleasure at having the 'opportunity of carrying into effect one of the grand objects of this Institution, the granting of honourable badges of distinction for successful exertions of valour; and, at the same time giving their personal testimony to the merit of those gallant achievements, which the trust delegated to them has made it their province to distinguish and reward.'

Turning to Captain Bissell and the two fathers: 'To you, Gentlemen, whose prowess

has added new triumphs to the British Flag, I shall not address myself in the language of panegyric: for modesty is ever allied to true courage. Your bravery stands recorded in the annals of your country, and in the hearts of your countrymen; a better tribute than the tongue can offer ... The Swords now to be presented to you, are the first honorary offering of an Institution, founded upon the patriotic motives of distinguishing those who signalise themselves, of alleviating the sufferings of those who are wounded, and of providing for the families of those who fall, in repelling or annoying our implacable foe.'

After further words in this vein, Marryat addressed Captain Bissell: 'On the part of the Committee of the Patriotic Fund, I present you this Sword, for the gallantry and professional abilities you displayed in engaging three French national vessels off Cumberland harbour, sent out for the express purpose of taking His Majesty's Sloop *Racoon*, then under your command. Your capturing those, who, confident in the superiority of their numbers, came out to capture you, is an action that speaks its own encomium more strongly than any words of mine can express it.'

In his reply, Captain Bissell thanked the Committee and hoped 'that the time is not

The contract for the production of the vases was given to the same company that had produced the presentation plate for Nelson after his victories at Aboukir Bay and Copenhagen, although its name had now changed to Rundell, Bridge and Rundell. They, in turn, asked John Flaxman to produce a design for a silver vase, which owed much to the prize-winning designs of John Shaw and Edward Edwards. Because of their commitments, they decided to subcontract the actual manufacture of the vases to a Mr Paul Storr and the firm of Smith & Scott. They were, like the swords, graded by value.

The first to be awarded was to Lieutenant Charles Pickford and was prompted, like many other awards, by a despatch from Captain Edward Dickson of HMS *Inconstant* published in *London Gazette*. On 7 March 1804, he had arrived off the island of Goree, which lies near the port of Dakar in present-day Senegal. Not certain whether the island was in French or British hands, although he did note that English colours were hoisted on the citadel and that the sentries had red coats, Dickson sent his First Lieutenant, Pickford, ashore in the cutter to check. Should Goree be in British hands, Pickford was to signal the ship.

At sunset, with no such signal received, Dickson ordered three boats, under the command of a midshipman, to go into the harbour and cut out any vessels that they might find. They succeeded in bringing out a ship under heavy fire from the batteries and learnt from its crew that the French had been in possession of the island for the past three weeks. The following day, Dickson, who also had a store ship and three other vessels under his command, positioned his squadron so that it could intercept any reinforcements sent from the mainland. He then began preparations for storming the citadel, including making scaling ladders. Matters were delayed, however, because his ships did not have sufficient boats to carry the number of men

far distant when I shall again be called forth into active service, so I shall look forward with more than common anxiety for an opportunity of wielding this Sword against the common enemy.' Captain Bowen, who was Commissioner of the Transport Board, then received his son's sword, which, he assured the Committee, would be forwarded to him at his current station, Jamaica.

Finally, it was Captain Watt's turn. He concluded his speech of thanks: 'This

Sword which you have now presented in so distinguished a manner, I trust my Boy will never disgrace: but when once drawn in the cause of his Country, it will not be sheathed without service to his King and honour to himself. On this occasion, I hope, Sir, you and the Gentlemen of the Committee will excuse those feelings of a Father which he is unable to express.' This was, however, the only time when the Committee presented swords in person.

that Dickson considered necessary to ensure success. A ship from the convoy that he appears to have been escorting arrived and the problem was overcome.

On the morning of 9 March, 'We were agreeably surprised by seeing the English colours hoisted over the French, and shortly after I received information from Lieutenant Pickford that the garrison had capitulated with [to] him.' So delighted was Dickson that he purchased 'a small brig' and sent it back to England, with Pickford in command, so that the Admiralty could be notified of the recapture of the island. This was common practice when a victory had been won, and a way of rewarding a deserving officer was to order him to carry the despatches, since it would bring him to the personal notice of the Lords of the Admiralty and, on occasion, the King or Prince of Wales.

In this instance, it was the Committee of the Patriotic Fund who took note. Having received a letter from William Marsden, the Secretary to the Admiralty, and after investigations by Thomson Bonar and John Julius Angerstein, the Committee decided at its regular weekly meeting on 15 May 1804 to award Pickford with a vase for his 'presence of mind, and address in negotiation' that induced the garrison to surrender. Unlike the later vase awards, no value was placed on Pickford's award, but its cost was just under £150. Midshipman James Hewitt, who had cut out the three vessels in the harbour, was awarded a £30 sword.

In the end, only one medal was ever awarded by the Patriotic Fund. The recipient was William Langfield, serving as a boy on board HM Sloop *Rattler*. During an action against French coastal batteries, a live shell landed on the main deck of the ship and was burning prior to exploding. Langfield gathered it in his hat and threw it overboard, 'by which,' in the words of his captain, 'the lives of many of the crew were saved; and

probably, the ship prevented from being blown up'. At its meeting on 3 July 1804, the Committee not only awarded Langfield a suitably inscribed medal, but also the sum of £20 'to be laid out in clothes and necessities, and that Captain Mason (Rattler's Captain) be requested to superintend the expenditure of the same'.

Another unique award was made to Mr John Marks. The Committee was informed in a letter from Lieutenant Henry Rowed, commanding HM Cutter *Sheerness*, that Marks, who was his boatswain, had successfully defended a *chasse-maree* (a type of French coasting vessel), which men of the *Sheerness* had just cut out from under the nose of a French coastal battery near Brest. The Committee considered the case on 18 October 1803 and awarded Marks an inscribed silver call and chain to the value of £10, a call being a bosun's whistle. The Fund also awarded two silver tankards during the first 15 months of its existence. The first, which was valued at £25, went to Mr William Nesbitt, Master of the Berwick smack *Queen Charlotte*, which had been armed by the government and had successfully fought off a French privateer early in 1804. Nesbitt himself was severely wounded and also received £50 in compensation.

The other award of a tankard caused the Committee some heart-searching. At its meeting on 9 October 1804, it considered a letter from the Bishop of Durham, which enclosed a statement signed by 'many of the Subscribers of that County'. It drew the attention of the Committee to the 'gallant conduct' of Mr Richard Robinson, Master of the collier *Scipio*, in beating off another privateer the previous April, an action in which he was severely wounded. Under the rules for granting awards from the Patriotic Fund, the defence of private property, which the collier was, was inadmissible. The Committee, however, recalled the Bishop's earlier letter concerning the subscriptions raised in Durham, which the donors originally wanted to use for local causes.

Bearing in mind that they had backed down and given the money over to the central fund, the Committee decided it would be churlish, in this case, to insist on a rigid application of the rules. Consequently, Mr Robinson received his tankard and £50 for his wounds.

In most cases, though, the Committee was very careful to apply the principle that acts of gallantry must be in defence of the country *per se*. In September 1803, it received a letter from Captain Thomas Chitty of the privateer *Earl Spencer*, which was based at Dover. In it he described an action between his ship and a French privateer in which two members of his crew, who were brothers, were wounded. He requested financial help for them. After some consideration, the request was turned down, since although privateers carried official letters of marque authorising them to engage enemy vessels, they existed primarily for personal gain.

Perhaps more problematical were the ships of the Honourable East India Company (HEIC). In November 1805, the Committee considered the case of one such vessel that had successfully defended herself against a French privateer. Yet, even though the Chairman and Deputy Chairman of the HEIC were members of the Committee, the request was rejected since the company was essentially a commercial organisation.

On the other hand, if regular warships engaged company ships, the Committee was prepared to think differently. Nathaniel Dance was Commodore of an East India Company convoy that left the Chinese port of Canton on 31 January 1804. It also included Britain-based merchant vessels. Two weeks later, as it entered the Straits of Malacca, the convoy was set upon by a French squadron consisting of an 84-gun battleship, two large frigates, a corvette, and a Dutch brig. While the company vessels did carry some armament, it was outmatched by that of the warships. The enemy ships

opened fire on the leading merchantmen, but, on Dance's instructions, these held their fire until the range grew shorter. Yet, soon after they had done so, the French ships turned away, probably under the mistaken impression that British warships were escorting the convoy. Dance pursued the enemy vessels for a short time, but conscious of the valuable cargoes that he was responsible for and that his new course was drawing him away from the Straits, he turned back and continued his passage. The Committee, clearly impressed by Dance's coolness in what was potentially a desperate situation, awarded him both a sword and a vase on the grounds of the 'new and peculiar lustre added to the British naval renown, by their [Dance and his fellow merchant captains] engaging and defeating a squadron of the enemy's men of war'. Indeed, so highly did the Patriotic Fund Committee regard the action of this convoy that they awarded £50 swords to the captains of all 15 East Indiamen present, and an additional £100 vase to Captain John Timins of the *Royal George*, which had born the brunt of the fighting. Furthermore, a naval officer who was a passenger aboard Dance's own vessel, the *Earl Camden*, also received a £50 sword. Dance himself was also knighted and received £5,000 from the Bombay Insurance Company, which was doubtless highly relieved not to have to face crippling claims on the loss of ships and their cargoes.

The Subscribers of Lloyd's as a whole also rewarded merchant skippers who had beaten off enemy attacks. Typical was the case of Captain Robert Hall of the Liverpool vessel *Fame*, who successfully drove off a 24-gun French corvette while sailing from Africa to Demerara and was presented with a silver tea service.

Lloyd's was also engaged in another project designed to help seafarers. This was the setting up of lifeboat stations around Britain's coasts. In 1790 there was a competition to build an unsinkable boat

for life-saving. Henry Greathead won it and his boat, named *Original*, became the first dedicated lifeboat and was based at South Shields. He was unsuccessful in obtaining money from parliament to build more and so Lloyd's stepped in. In May 1802, they voted him an award of 100 guineas and set aside the sum of £2,000 from corporate funds to assist in the construction of lifeboats to the Greathead design elsewhere. This project continued through the Napoleonic Wars and beyond and by 1825 there were 25 lifeboat stations in existence.

Back to the Patriotic Fund, the Committee was especially careful when it came to making grants to the families of those whom had died in the service of their country. The very first of these awards were made on 7 October 1803 and concerned the hired armed cutter *Princess Augusta*, which had fought a desperate battle against two Dutch schooners. The Committee was made aware of this, both through a despatch from Admiral Montague, which was published in the *London Gazette*, and a letter from the Master of the ship, Joseph Thomas.

The Committee's first action in cases like this was to obtain a list of killed and wounded. In this instance, the commanding officer of the *Princess Augusta*, Lieutenant Scott, was killed during the action and Thomas took over command. They awarded Scott's widow an annuity of £30 for life, but also noted that she was pregnant. They therefore granted the unborn child an annuity of £10 until he or she reached the age of 21. In the event, Mrs Scott gave birth to a boy. The widow of the ship's boatswain was granted a £15 annuity for life, and that of the gunner £20. One seaman who was wounded, and had a wife and child, was given £20 and another wounded seaman £10. Joseph Thomas himself was rewarded with £200 'for fighting bravely after the loss of his Commanding Officer'.

The first case concerning a soldier was brought before the Committee on 22

November 1803. A letter from the commanding officer of the 8th Loyal North London Volunteers sought assistance for the widow of one of his men who had been accidentally killed on duty. J J Angerstein personally investigated and the woman was granted a £25 annuity. In contrast, an application on behalf of the widow of member of the Navy's Impress Service, who was killed while attempting to impress a seaman at Exmouth, was deemed ineligible. So was that for a widow, with children, whose husband had fallen from the rigging of HMS *Royal Sovereign*.

While pressing a man into Naval Service might well not fall within the strict definition of defence of country, making the rejection understandable, one can only assume that the unfortunate sailor fell to his death through his own carelessness and that the Committee decided that this did not entitle his widow to help from the Fund. Alas, the minutes do not provide any explanation.

Clearly this was not the case with Lieutenant Thomas Parsons of HMS *Hecate*, who drowned when his boat capsized; his widow received a £20 annuity. The Committee were, however, quite emphatic that, in cases of death, money would only be given to dependants. When the Mayor of Plymouth requested financial assistance for the sister of an officer killed on board HMS *Goliath*, the Committee had no hesitation in turning him down. It transpired that she was married to a doctor and had not been financially dependent on her brother.

On 8 May 1804, a week after the Committee had considered this case, it had in front of it three petitions. The first was from the commanding officer of the Sea Fencibles at Aldeburgh. The Sea Fencibles were a part-time force, raised from among fishermen and other local seamen, whose role was coast defence. In this instance, three of their number had been drowned while attempting to get off a ship in distress. The request for financial help for their dependants was turned down, presumably because they were not on duty at the time.

This supposition is reinforced by an earlier case concerning the Sea Fencibles. On this occasion, they had been carrying out practice firings from some newly established batteries at Cromer. Unfortunately, a shot from the easternmost battery struck the westernmost battery, severely wounding Captain Tremlett RN, who was in command, and necessitating the immediate amputation of a surgeon's leg. The Committee awarded Tremlett £400, but dismissed the claim on behalf of the surgeon on the grounds that he had been a mere spectator and was not officially on duty.

As for the two other petitions considered at the 8 May meeting, the Committee rejected one from a captain on behalf of a seaman who had lost two fingers of his right hand, possibly because this injury was not considered to be incapacitating. The other was the sad case of a woman who had lost her only son from yellow fever in Jamaica and whose husband was serving in the East Indies. Again, the Committee turned down her plea, probably on the grounds that her husband, even though he was far away, could support her financially.

Even so, the Patriotic Fund was making many more awards than it was rejecting. To encourage applications, details of the awards were circulated among the Fleet. One the most enthusiastic supporters of the Fund was Horatio Nelson. He had seen at first hand the welfare benefits of the earlier Lloyd's subscriptions, some of which were still in existence and continuing to deal with cases arising out of the various actions that they commemorated.

Once the Patriotic Fund was instituted, Nelson's correspondence with Angerstein resumed. On 24 March 1804, he wrote to

Angerstein from HMS *Victory* at sea in reply to a letter from the latter concerning the particulars of a seaman killed on board the sloop *Morgiana*: '... you will please acquaint the Committee that I have given a general order to return the names and families of all the Officers and men who have been, or may be, killed or wounded, on board the different Ships under my command'. Furthermore, Nelson gave instructions that every wounded man leaving one of his ships was to be furnished with a certificate describing his wounds and signed by the captain and surgeon.

Another keen supporter was Sir Sydney Smith, hero of the defence of Acre in 1799, who wrote to the Committee recommending the officers and crews of HM Ships *Antelope* and *Magicienne* for their capture of a Dutch vessel in March 1804. This resulted in the award of £50 swords to two lieutenants of the *Antelope* and a £30 sword to a midshipman of the *Magicienne*.

There is no doubt that the Patriotic Fund was already a source of encouragement, especially for the Royal Navy. Indeed, this first phase of the new war was a tense time. Britain stood without allies and in the knowledge that across the English Channel Napoleon was actively engaged in preparing an invasion. Only the Royal Navy could prevent him and this condemned many of its ships to the monotonous business of the blockade. Try as they might, the British Admirals, including Nelson now off Toulon, could not tempt the French ships out so that they could engage them in open battle. Other squadrons were deployed farther afield, protecting British possessions overseas. In the words of the famous American naval historian Alfred Mahan, 'Those far distant, storm-beaten ships, upon which the Grand Army never looked, stood between it and domination of the world.' In 1805, however, the pace would quicken and the calls on the Patriotic Fund increase.

Chapter Three

THE YEAR OF TRAFALGAR 1805

The beginning of 1805 saw Nelson still trying to tempt the French fleet out of Toulon so that he could engage it in open battle. While, in the Atlantic, Cornwallis maintained a close blockade of Brest. He was also forced to deploy a squadron to Ferrol because of the Spanish declaration of war against Britain in November 1804. Across the English Channel, Napoleon's *Grande Armée* remained waiting for a favourable situation to develop at sea to allow an invasion.

The first significant action took place, however, not in the Mediterranean or Atlantic, but in the West Indies. On 22 February, a squadron of ships appeared off the town of Roseau on the coast of Dominica. They were flying British colours, but came too close to one of the forts. Brigadier George Prevost, commanding the troops, ordered his guns to open fire and at that moment a number of 'large barges' began to head for the shore. The ships then broke out the French colours.

Men of the 1st West India and 46th Regiments, and the local militia, repulsed the initial attempts to land, but were forced to withdraw when they came under the fire of some of the French ships. The French duly landed and, in spite of some gallant counterattacks, Prevost found himself outgunned by the French ships. Determined to maintain sovereignty over at least part of Dominica, Prevost withdrew his troops by forced march to St Rupert's on the other side of the island.

The garrison there had previously been warned by Prevost of the French landings and had done much to put St Rupert's in an effective state of defence. The French force re-embarked from Roseau on the 27th, after 'levying a contribution', and appeared off St Rupert's on the same day. The French commander sent a surrender demand ashore, warning Prevost that he risked the same destruction as had befallen Roseau. The British commander replied: 'I have had the honour to receive your Letter. My duty to my King and Country is so superior to every other consideration, that I have only to thank you for the observations you have been pleased to make on the often inevitable consequences of war.' Faced with this elegant rebuff, the French withdrew to Guadaloupe.

This was the first proper military action to come before the Patriotic Fund Committee and in May they considered Prevost's despatch, as published in the *London Gazette* with a covering letter from the overall British commander in the West Indies, General Sir William Myers. They were impressed by Prevost's performance and awarded him not only a £100 sword, but also 'a piece of Plate to the value of Two Hundred Pounds, with appropriate inscriptions ... for the distinguished gallantry and military talents he displayed on that occasion, by which the sovereignty of the Island was preserved to His Majesty's arms'.

Two of his officers, both of whom were wounded, were also rewarded with swords and plate, although of lesser value. Another wounded officer was awarded £100, and

£40 went to each man who had received a disabling wound or had suffered the loss of a limb. Other men severely wounded were given £20 and those with slight wounds £10.

Attention remained focused on the West Indies. Napoleon had drawn up a new plan designed to fox the Royal Navy and provide him with the necessary superiority in the English Channel so that his invasion could take place. He gave orders for his fleets at Toulon and Brest to break out and sail for the West Indies, with that at Brest picking up the Spanish squadron based at Ferrol *en route*. They were to rendezvous at Martinique and create as much havoc as possible among the British possessions in the Caribbean. The Combined Fleets were then to sail back across the Atlantic and sweep up the English Channel.

Admiral Pierre Villeneuve, commanding at Toulon, slipped anchor on 30 March. He succeeded in evading Nelson and passed through the Straits of Gibraltar under the cover of a gale, arriving off Cadiz on 9 April. The small British squadron covering the Spanish port was taken by surprise and withdrew to warn the Ferrol and Brest blockading forces. Now joined by Spanish ships, Villeneuve vanished into the Atlantic. As for the French fleet in Brest, the blockade was too tight for it to risk venturing out and it decided to await Villeneuve's return from the West Indies.

As soon as he realised that Villeneuve had escaped him, Nelson decided to patrol between Sardinia and the African coast.

He feared that his adversary was bound either for Egypt or Italy. Then, on 10 April, he learnt that a British convoy was *en route* for Italy, where it was to land troops to cooperate with the Russians. This was a result of lengthy negotiations that the British Government was having in St Petersburg in its efforts to persuade Russia to re-enter the war. Fearing that the convoy was Villeneuve's target, Nelson sailed westwards. Contrary winds slowed him and he did not reach Gibraltar until 5 May. In the meantime, he had ascertained that Villeneuve had linked up with the Spanish and had continued to sail westwards.

His initial belief was that the Combined Fleet was bound for Ireland or the Channel, but further evidence began to point to the West Indies. Waiting to ensure that the troop convoy, which had been sheltering in the mouth of the River Tagus, was safely through the Straits of Gibraltar, Nelson made up his mind and set sail once more, reaching Madeira on 14 May, where he knew he could pick up the trade winds which would carry him across the Atlantic. From here he sent a letter back to the Admiralty explaining his intention. In London, too, the conclusion reached was that Villeneuve was bound for the West Indies and Nelson's letter was received with relief.

The Franco-Spanish fleet arrived at Martinique on 13 May. Villeneuve was still hoping that Admiral Ganteaume would join him with the Brest fleet and, if this was not to be, expected orders recalling him to Europe. Consequently, he undertook no major operations to wrest islands off the

British until on 4 June he was joined by two further ships, which brought orders for him to await Ganteaume for five more weeks. If he had not arrived by the end of this period, Villeneuve was to sail for Ferrol. In the meantime, he was to occupy as many British islands as possible.

Nelson arrived off Tobago two days later, having made an exceptionally fast passage across the Atlantic, and was determined to engage Villeneuve, even though his ten ships were outnumbered by more than two to one. Villeneuve meanwhile had set about preparing to seize the small island of Barbuba, northernmost of the Leeward Islands. While en route, he fell in with a convoy of sugar ships, capturing 14 of them. To his horror, he learnt from the crews that Nelson had anchored off Barbados four days before. Rather than risk meeting him, Villeneuve set sail for Ferrol.

Nelson did not receive firm news of this until 12 June, four days later, when the schooner which had been escorting the sugar convoy informed him that the whole of the Combined Fleet, now 32 ships strong, had last been seen sailing northeast. Nelson at once despatched a sloop to England with the message that he was in pursuit. He sent another vessel with the same message to warn Admiral Calder, who was off Ferrol.

The sloop *Curieux* arrived back in England and, on the night of 9 July, her captain brought additional news to the Admiralty that he had passed the Combined Fleet and that, from its course, it appeared to be making for the Bay of Biscay. Admiral Sir Charles Barham, the First Sea Lord, immediately wrote orders. Cornwallis was to carry out a cruise of the Bay and then resume his bottling up of Ganteaume. The squadron blockading Rochefort was to join Calder off Ferrol. The two joined up on 15 July and sailed out into the Atlantic to intercept Villeneuve.

This they did seven days later, but the weather was murky and it was not until towards evening that the two fleets clashed. Calder captured two Spanish ships, but one three-decker, *Windsor Castle*, lost her mainmast. Conscious of the threat posed by the French ships at Rochefort and Ferrol to his rear, Calder did not resume the action on the following day and Villeneuve was able to slip into the Spanish port of Vigo. He sailed again on 31 July and, taking advantage of a gale which blew Calder off station, entered Ferrol two days later.

Awaiting Villeneuve were orders from Napoleon to leave immediately and join up with Ganteaume, whom Napoleon had been badgering to leave Brest, and/or the Rochefort squadron, which had left port to make a diversion off Ireland. At the same time, the *Grande Armée* was poised to cross the English Channel, with Napoleon himself arriving at Boulogne on 3 August.

As for Nelson, he reached Gibraltar on 19 July. After revictualling his ships, he was awaiting a favourable wind when he received a Lisbon paper with an account of the intelligence gained by the *Curieux*. He therefore set sail for England, not even stopping to communicate with Collingwood, who was still blockading Cadiz.

On 13 August Villeneuve sailed from Ferrol. He sent out a frigate to make contact with the Rochefort squadron, but she was captured by a British frigate. The Rochefort squadron then returned to Vigo. Calder, realising that Villeneuve had got out of Ferrol, sailed north and joined Cornwallis, as did Admiral Stirling, who had been blockading Rochefort. On 15 August Nelson also joined off Ushant, making a total strength of 39 ships. Villeneuve, who had become increasingly pessimistic, soon realised that he was in danger of being annihilated. He therefore withdrew to Cadiz, a timely gale enabling him to evade Collingwood.

The meticulous logbook of the Frigate HMS Euralyus for 21 October 1805, including a note of Nelson's famous Trafalgar signal: 'England expects every man to do his duty.' The logbook was the responsibility of the ship's Master, who was also in charge of navigation.

Photograph: © LLOYD'S

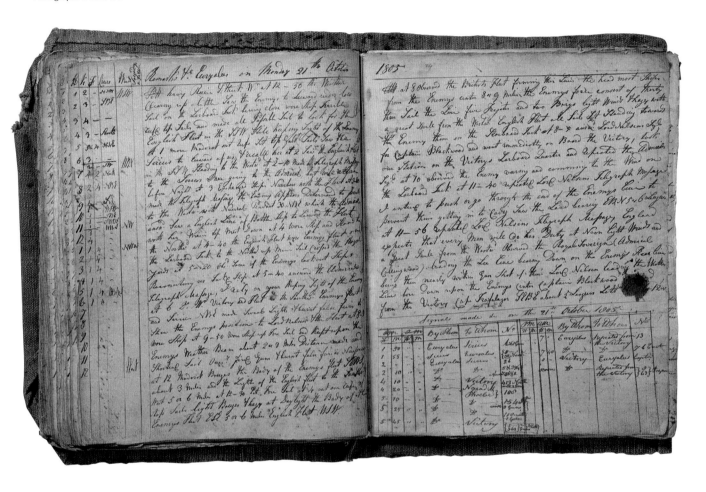

Having obtained Cornwallis's permission, Nelson now returned to England in his flagship HMS *Victory* accompanied by just one other ship. To a country that felt very much under the threat of imminent invasion, he was seen as a saviour. In spite, of his abortive chase of Villeneuve across the Atlantic and back, he was still 'England's darling'.

John Julius Angerstein probably hoped that the Admiral might make another visit to Lloyd's, but it was not to be. In the meantime, the Patriotic Fund continued its weekly meetings. On 27 August, it had in front of it lists of casualties from Calder's inconclusive action off Cape Finisterre some five weeks earlier and made several awards to those wounded

and to the widows of those killed. As was the Committee's standard practice, money given to the latter was at the discretion of the ministers of their local parishes. No honorary awards were made for the Cape Finisterre encounter, probably because the general public had castigated Calder for his failure to renew the action, thus allowing Villeneuve to slip away.

The case of Lieutenant George Pickford of HMS *Cumbrian* was considered at the same meeting. For his part in the capture of a Spanish privateer schooner on 13 June he was awarded a £50 sword. Just over three weeks later and, while in command of another prize, he seized three further vessels. The Committee awarded him a £100 vase for this second display of zeal.

Nelson leaves Portsmouth for the last time, 14 September 1805, by Andrew Garrick Gow (1848-1920). It is inaccurate in that he actually embarked from Southsea beach, but the mood is evocative.
Painting: © LLOYD'S

The fact that Admiral Villeneuve had allowed himself to become bottled up once more and far away from the English Channel radically changed Napoleon's strategic perceptions. He realised that he no longer had the means to achieve the local naval supremacy necessary for an invasion. Napoleon was also well aware that Pitt's efforts to form another coalition had finally succeeded and both Russia and Austria had now allied themselves to Britain and were preparing to take to the offensive both in Germany and northern Italy.

Consequently, he turned his eyes eastwards. His intention was to defeat Austria and Russia in detail and to bring the whole of Italy under his sway. During the last days of August his armies began to dowse their camp fires on the North Sea and Channel coasts and set off for Germany. Napoleon himself, having ordered Villeneuve to break out from Cadiz and enter the Mediterranean so as to support the impending operations in Italy, left Boulogne on 2 September.

News of this quickly reached England. Simultaneously, Captain Henry Blackwood in the frigate *Euryalus* brought news of the Combined Fleet in Cadiz. On his way to the Admiralty, Blackwood called in on Nelson at his house at Merton, near Wimbledon, prompting Nelson himself to hurry to London on the following day. The intelligence that Blackwood brought implied that Cadiz was not well enough stocked with provisions to maintain the Combined Fleet and that this would force it into the open sea.

The decision was made that Nelson was to reassume command of the Mediterranean Fleet and take Collingwood under his wing. Time was now of the essence. Within a week *Victory* had been revictualled and on the night of 13 September, having dined for the last time with his beloved Emma Hamilton, Nelson left Merton for Portsmouth. He wrote in his diary: 'May the great God whom I adore enable me to fulfil the expectations of my country.'

Nelson boarded *Victory* on the following day, crowds threatening to swamp him as he stepped on to his barge at Southsea beach, which he had selected rather than the normal landing stage. On 15 September, accompanied by *Euryalus*, the flagship weighed anchor. Thirteen days later, Nelson joined Collingwood. He deployed his fleet well below the horizon, relying on his frigates to act as his eyes.

Among the many memoranda that he sent to his captains during the next few weeks, one read: 'It is my particular directions that the name and family of every Officer, Seaman, and Marine, who may be killed or wounded in Action with the Enemy, on board any of His Majesty's Ships and Vessels under my command, be returned to me as soon as possible as soon after the circumstance happens, as the Service will admit of, agreeable to the annexed Form, in order that I may transmit it to the Chairman of the Patriotic Fund at Lloyd's Coffee-house, that the case of the relations of those that may fall in the cause of their Country may be taken into consideration.'

In the meantime, Villeneuve and his Spanish ally initially refused to obey Napoleon's order to break out, believing that the British fleet was too strong. A furious Napoleon ordered him to be replaced as commander of the Combined Fleet. Realising that many of his ships were getting short of provisions, Nelson ordered six under Admiral Sir Thomas Louis to Gibraltar and Tetuan to replenish. Louis was not happy: 'You are sending us away, my Lord – the Enemy will come out, and we shall have no share in the Battle.' Nelson sought to reassure him, but events would prove Louis correct in his prophecy.

Villeneuve learned on 18 October that his successor had arrived in Madrid. At the same time came news that Louis and his six ships had put into Gibraltar. Believing that, if he allowed himself to be replaced without taking any positive action, he would be branded a coward, he decided to take advantage of Nelson's now slightly weakened fleet and put to sea.

Early on 19 October, the frigate *Sirius* signalled that the French and Spanish ships had their topsails hoisted. An hour later they began to leave port. Nelson shadowed Villeneuve, keeping his ships out of sight and continuing to rely on his frigates. Visibility was initially poor and for a time Nelson feared that his adversary might have returned to port. Nevertheless, Nelson manoeuvred so that he could guard the approaches to the Straits of Gibraltar. Clearer weather in the afternoon of 20 October confirmed that Villeneuve was still at sea and on course.

Nelson had already made his plans and briefed his captains for the battle. He intended to form two columns to break the enemy's line and anticipated that as soon as Villeneuve spotted the British, he would abandon his attempt to get through the Straits and withdraw back to Cadiz.

On the morning of the following day the British columns, the northerly led by Nelson and the other by Collingwood, closed by degrees on the Combined Fleet which, as Nelson had correctly predicated had altered course to the north. Villeneuve had been concerned, not just by Nelson's appearance, but also the threat presented by Admiral Louis in the Straits themselves. At 11.48am signal flags broke out on *Victory's* yardarm: 'England expects every man to do his duty'. The French and the Spanish fired the first shots and Victory made another signal: 'Engage the enemy more closely'. Battle was then joined.

Trafalgar has been described many times. Suffice to say that Nelson's tactics worked well, but that he himself was mortally wounded by a musket ball an hour and a half after the action began and died three hours later while the fighting continued. Of the 33 ships of the Combined Fleet,

19 struck their colours and nearly 9,000 French and Spanish sailors were killed or wounded. The total British casualties were 1,690.

Collingwood, who had assumed command on Nelson's death, was now faced with the task of shepherding the captured ships, many of them so battered that they had to be put under tow, and his own fleet, which had also sustained damage, to Gibraltar. Then a gale blew up, which lasted for seven days. It soon became clear that to continue to tow the damaged prizes would place his own ships in danger. Consequently, Collingwood ordered the majority of the captured ships to be destroyed and only four were brought into Gibraltar. As for the surviving French and Spanish ships, ten managed to reach the safety of Cadiz, but never left port again, while the other four were intercepted and captured by Sir Richard Strachan off the Spanish coast at Ferrol on 4 November.

Not until 6 November did the news of Trafalgar reach an England reeling from recent reports that Napoleon had defeated and forced the surrender of an Austrian Army under General Mack at Ulm. Nelson's death overshadowed the fact that a brilliant victory had been won, and the Underwriters at Lloyd's wept openly when they heard of it.

The Committee of the Patriotic Fund considered the matter on 14 November, having in front of them Collingwood's despatch and news of Strachan's success off Ferrol. It was clear from the first reports of casualties that there would be heavy calls on the Fund. Indeed, up until 6 November, the total money raised stood at £195,000, of which £50,000 had already been paid out in awards. The Committee therefore agreed to make a public announcement:

'To meet the claims of the numerous Sufferers in these memorable engagements, with a liberality proportional to their heroic achievements, will so reduce the present Fund as may leave an inadequate provision for future instances of British Valour.

The Committee are aware that many have withheld their Subscriptions to the general Purposes of this Institution, who have been accustomed to subscribe on particular occasions; that others may have deferred them under the idea that the Sum already raised would prove equal to any possible exigency. It is hoped that all these will now come forward; and while with solemn Thanksgivings we acknowledge the Interposition of divine providence, let us also remember the Sufferings of those who were the Instruments of this signal manifestation of its Favour to these Kingdoms.'

In addition, the King declared that 5 December was to be a day of national thanksgiving and it was agreed that church collections on that day would be for the benefit of the Patriotic Fund. This raised more than £77,000 and another £43,400 was forthcoming in subscriptions. The Committee could therefore feel more confident that it would be able to meet its sharply increased commitments.

Yet, on 3 December, hardly before any money had come in, the Committee had agreed on a scale of awards. It voted £500 vases to Nelson's widow and his surviving brother William, who had been ennobled as Earl Nelson of Trafalgar in recognition of Horatio's service to his country, as well as one to Collingwood. Vases to the value of £300 were awarded to Strachan and Rear Admiral The Earl of Northesk, who had been third in command at Trafalgar.

All serving captains and commanders of ships present at either Trafalgar or Ferrol would receive £100 swords, although some, including Nelson's Flag Captain, Thomas Hardy, chose to accept vases of the same value instead. The widows of the captains of HMS *Bellerophon* and *Mars*, who were killed at Trafalgar, also received vases.

Only two captains, Eliab Harvey of HMS *Temeraire* and Edward Codrington of HMS *Orion*, were not honoured by the Fund. Codrington certainly declined because he wanted the money spent on the wounded and the same probably applied to Harvey. The Committee initially overlooked one entitled officer, Lieutenant Robert Young, commanding HM Cutter *Entreprenante*. In May 1806 he wrote to John Welsford, Secretary to the Patriotic Fund, pointing out that his ship had been present at Trafalgar and 'suffer'd so considerable from the number of Prisoners She had on board consisting of One hundred and Sixty Nine Men I pick'd up from the La' Achille (that Blew up) with little or no water on board during all the Gales'. The Committee duly awarded him his sword. One junior officer not in command of a ship was also the subject of an honorary award. Lieutenant Simons of HMS *Defiance* had boarded the French ship L'*Aigle*, wounded her captain, and then hauled down her colours. He was then killed in the act of hauling up the British colours in their place. The Committee awarded a £100 vase to his father.

At the 3 December meeting, the Committee also considered what financial awards should be made to the wounded. It decided to apply the same categories of rank used when distributing prize money. In these circumstances, they were divided into classes:

❖ First class: captains and commanders of ships
❖ Second class: naval lieutenants and captains of marines
❖ Third class: warrant officers, boatswain, gunners, carpenters, pursers, chaplains, surgeons, lieutenants of marines
❖ Fourth class: petty officers, midshipmen, boatswain's and gunner's mates, clerks, masters-of-arms, and ships' tradesmen (sailmakers, caulkers, ropemakers)
❖ Fifth class: the remainder.

The Committee drew up its scale for grants of money as follows:

	Severely wounded	Slightly wounded
2nd class	£100	£50
3rd class	£50	£30
4th class	£40	£25
5th class	£20	£10

In addition, those of the fifth class who lost a limb would be awarded £40 and, although never formally agreed by the Committee, those in the other classes who suffered disabling wounds were also awarded twice the sum given for a severe wound. Nelson had already instilled in his captains the need to furnish the Patriotic Fund with details of those among their crews who had been killed or wounded. The Committee now had to wait for these lists to come in. Only then would it decide what should be done about dependants of those who had been killed.

The lists themselves, which were signed by the captain and ship's surgeon, made grim reading. Captain Hardy recorded the names of 57 killed, 25 dangerously wounded, 13 badly wounded, and 41 slightly wounded on board *Victory*. HMS *Britannia* suffered ten killed and 41 wounded, and *Revenge* 28 and 53. *Bellorophon* had a total of 156 casualties, but the highest number was incurred by *Colossus*, which had 48 killed and 151 wounded. The Fund paid out an initial total of £2,565 to help her wounded, while those on board *Victory* received £1,625.

In total, £25,765 was dispersed to help the wounded of both Trafalgar and Ferrol. The Committee sent out bills of exchange to each captain, who then cashed them, paid out the men, obtained their signatures on receipt and returned these to John Welsford, the Secretary. It was inevitable that it took time to trace some men, especially when a ship was paid off and they were transferred to

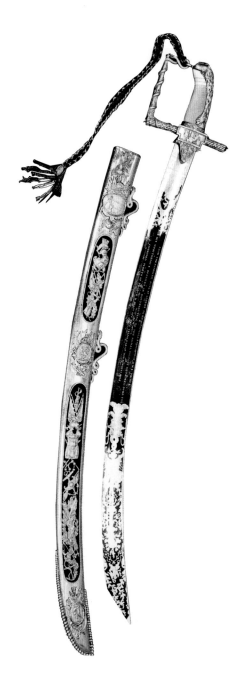

other vessels. Captains, however, did
their best to keep the Fund informed.
In some cases the captains had themselves
been posted and the new captain was not
prepared to vouch for men who had been
wounded. This happened to four seamen
of HMS *Temeraire*. Eliab Harvey was
promoted Rear Admiral and the new
captain would have nothing to do with
their claims, even though the ship's surgeon
interceded. For some reason, he refused to
issue them 'smart tickets'; the vouchers that
would enable them to be paid an allowance
by the Navy Office for their wounds. The
four men were then posted to HMS
Inconstant, whose captain also showed them
no consideration. In desperation, they
wrote to Harvey, who put pressure on the
surgeon. The result was that the men did
each receive the £10 due to them from the
Fund for being slightly wounded.

There were also men who were sent to help
man the prizes and did not return to their
own ships. Captain Conn of HMS *Dreadnought*
wrote to Welsford in March 1806,
explaining that he had had six of these
men, all injured while aboard the prizes.
Sadly, one had died in the meantime and
the others came from three different ships.
The Fund duly made monetary awards to
the five survivors.

There were also delays in paying those
men admitted to hospital. Almost a year
after the battle, Captain John Lumley, on
board the sloop HMS *Paulina* off the Dutch
Texel, wrote to Welsford drawing his
attention to one Seaman George Hewitt,
a member of his crew who had been aboard
Temeraire at Trafalgar and had been badly
wounded in the thigh and breast. Because he
was in the naval hospital at Haslar at the time
the awards were announced, he never
received his and Lumley wanted to know
how he could obtain it.

Some captains and surgeons drew the
Committee's attention to individual acts
of bravery and self-sacrifice. Luke Nagle,

surgeon to HMS *Neptune*, described how
Seaman Felix McCarthy was struck in the
arm by a cannon ball during the battle and
was brought down for Nagle to attend to
him. Immediately afterwards, another badly
wounded man was brought in. McCarthy
told Nagle to deal with him first. The
surgeon then amputated McCarthy's arm
and he returned to his battle station.

'I have no doubt but this Man's good
Conduct will procure him a Cook's Warrant
through his Captain's recommendation
which appears to be the height of this Poor
Fellow's Ambition in order to support an
Aged Father & Mother.' McCarthy duly
received his cook's warrant and £40 from
the Fund for the loss of his arm.

Captain Sir Thomas Thompson submitted
a letter of recommendation on behalf of an
old shipmate, who had been a member of
his crew when he commanded HMS *Bellona*
at Copenhagen in 1801. He had since been
present at Calder's action off Cape Finisterre
in July 1805 and at Trafalgar, where he had
been badly wounded in the leg, from which
'he has suffer'd greatly & added to the
patience, endures the poverty of Job'.
He enclosed a cutting from the *Gibraltar
Chronicle* of January 1806, which described
how this man, James Spratt, who was Mate
of HMS *Defiance*, had led a boarding party
about the French *Aigle*. He got aboard the
enemy vessel by swimming between the
two ships and using *Aigle's* rudder chains.

Unfortunately, his boarders,
misunderstanding his orders, did not
follow him. Undaunted, Spratt tried to haul
down the ship's colours, but was attacked by
several men, whom he successfully repelled.
The ships were now close enough for the
remainder of the boarders to get across and
they attacked a French officer, who cried for
mercy. Spratt covered him with his body and
saved his life, but while continuing to
protect the Frenchman a musket was aimed
at his chest. He managed to deflect it, but
not enough to prevent the ball entering his

Part of HMS Victory's return of killed and wounded at Trafalgar. These lists enabled the Patriotic Fund to give financial assistance to the wounded and the dependants of the dead. *Photograph: © LLOYD'S*

leg, badly fracturing it. Still on the ground, he found himself grappling with two more Frenchmen, who were then despatched by his fellow boarders. In this case, the Committee awarded Spratt an additional £30 on top of the £50 that he had already been granted.

Captain Henry Bayntun (*Leviathan*) told of one of his seamen, whose arm had been shattered, insisting that others be treated before him and then singing 'with a steady clear voice' the whole of *Rule Britannia* while the remains of his limb were being amputated. 'The cheerfulness of this tough Son of Neptune has been of infinite use in keeping up the spirits of the Wounded, his Shipmates, and I hope and trust the recital of this little story will be of service to him.' Sadly, the man succumbed to fever in the hospital at Gibraltar before any award could be made.

There were some sad individual cases. An anonymous lady wrote to the wife of George Munro, a member of the Patriotic Fund Committee, enclosing a memorial from Mrs Charlotte Scott, the widow of Nelson's secretary on board Victory. She had spent the day with Mrs Scott, 'but to describe the State of mind she is still in, is beyond my power – your own feelings will convey an idea of the sufferings of a lovely Young Woman, in one moment forever deprived of a Husband She ador'd, and the Father of her children'.

Scott had spent two years aboard the ship without having seen his family and, if he had survived Trafalgar, would have been given a lucrative shore job as 'Agent for All

the Prizes'. As it was, Mrs Scott was left with three boys all under the age of 11 and, as she wrote herself, 'with very inadequate means for their Maintenance and Education'. The Committee was clearly moved, but was not clear as to how an admiral's secretary stood with regard to the prize money classifications of rank. Conscious of the need to observe the rules that it had laid down for itself, the Committee therefore sought the advice of Scott's executors. They pointed out that technically an admiral's secretary stood only in the third class when it came to prize money. However, his pay of £300 per annum was considerably more than that of the likes of boatswain and gunners and what would suffice for their widows would not do so for a secretary's widow. They also pointed out that it was common practice for commanders-in-chief to appoint their secretaries agents for the prizes they captured 'and there are few instances where Secretaries to commanders in Chief have not in this way acquired an independent property'.

The problem was that they could not think of an instance over the past 100 years of an admiral's secretary being killed in action and so there was no precedent to follow. As it was, they estimated that Scott's estate was worth some £400 per annum and also enclosed a letter written by Nelson to Scott on their return to England in August 1805. It read: 'I cannot allow myself to part from you even (as I hope) for a very short time without giving you the assurance of my sincere esteem and regard, and to say that as a secretary for ability, punctuality and regularity that I believe your superior is not to be met with, and as a Gentleman that your own Conduct has been most exemplary during the whole time you have been with me.' The Committee was reassured and granted Mrs Scott a £60 annuity that was to pass to her children on her death.

John Brown, father of a boy killed at Trafalgar, wrote to Welsford: 'I have myself been forty two years in the Service of His Majesty (as a Shipwright), part of the time at Sea, am fifty five years of age, my Wife fifty two; have brought up five children, three of whom have served in the Navy – the youngest (aged fifteen years & nine months), fell in the late memorable Action, while most gallantly exerting himself in cutting away the rigging of an Enemy's Ship that had fallen on board the Tonnant. I have a Son & Daughter yet unprovided for, & as I am rather in indigent circumstances, any thing the Committee may bestow will be most gratefully receiv'd. His Mothers' distress on the melancholy occasion it is not in my power to describe, her Grief is unceasing & occasions the liveliest apprehensions for her safety, the only consolation I can feel for the loss of so promising a son, is the glorious manner in which he fell & the handsome way he is spoken of by his Captain & Officers.' Again, the Committee must have been moved by this appeal and awarded Mr Brown £80.

In other cases, the Committee turned down requests. One was on behalf of the late Lieutenant William Ram, who was also killed on board Victory. A friend of the family wrote to ask if the Fund would grant a sum of money to his father, who was a colonel in the Army and the Member of Parliament for County Wexford in Ireland, for the erection of 'some small tablet or monument' which would be dedicated to Lieutenant Ram's memory. This lay totally outside the scope of the Patriotic Fund and the Committee had little difficulty in rejecting it.

In one or two cases, captains refused to pass on awards made from the Fund. Captain Lawrence Halsted declined to hand over the £20 granted to Seaman Patrick O'Keefe on the grounds that he was 'a most notorious thief, and in every respect undeserving such an award'. There was, too, certainly one case in which a false claim was made. At its meeting on 20 January 1807, the Committee noted that one John Dermott had pretended to have been wounded on board Leviathan at Trafalgar and was now to be prosecuted for fraud.

In one case, the Committee confused an officer's rank. John Pasco, Nelson's Flag Lieutenant who persuaded him to alter 'Nelson confides' to 'England expects' in his famous pre-Trafalgar signal because the former would use too many signal flags, was wounded in the arm during the battle and was awarded £100 by the Patriotic Fund. In March 1806 he wrote to the Fund stating that the original assumption was that he would make a full recovery. However, his arm was 'now more ornamental than useful, and I am fearful I shall never have the use of it again'. As a result, it had 'rather embarrassed me in pecuniary matters'. He also enclosed a surgeon's certificate.

It would seem that the Fund considered that he had been given a sufficient award for, on 25 June, Pasco wrote again. He complained that he had been addressed as 'Lieutenant M Pasco Royal Marines', when in fact he had been promoted Commander RN after Trafalgar and was entitled to be addressed as 'Captain'. He feared that this error had caused him to be considered as part of the third class, especially since he knew of captains of Royal Marines who had received £200 for disabling wounds. The fact that the Navy Office had granted him a five shillings per diem disability pension also proved the seriousness of his wound. He also submitted a certificate signed this time by three surgeons. The Committee relented and Pasco received an additional £100.

What this revealed was that officers in the second class were being awarded twice as much as the Committee had originally laid down, and the same also applied to some at least of the third class. The Fund also made additional awards to other cases in which wounds proved more serious than first thought.

Given the slowness of communications, the Patriotic Fund and the Royal Navy did remarkably well in settling almost all claims by the late summer of 1806. But others continued to trickle through. Two cases considered in 1808 concerned women and act as a reminder of the fact that the Navy in Nelson's day did permit a certain number of wives to be on board, not just in port, but at sea as well. Two of these were Mrs Ellis Armstrong and Charlotte Pannel of HMS *Swiftsure* to whom the Fund awarded sums of £10 and £5 for their dedication in helping look after those members of the crew who were wounded at Trafalgar.

The year 1805 turned out to be a particularly busy one for the Patriotic Fund, not least because it became involved in another field of charitable works. The minutes of a meeting held on 25 June recorded: 'Read a Letter from Paul Le Mesurier, Esq. Inclosing an extract of one received from Captain Brenton, late of HMS *Minerve*, dated Verdun the 12th May; recommending to the consideration of the Committee, the distressed situation of the English prisoners of war in France, and stating, that the Funds by which an Hospital for the relief of the sick and wounded had hitherto been supported, were now exhausted.'

There were three types of prisoners. First were the officers and crews of Royal Navy ships that had been captured by the French, as well as a few soldiers. Crews of merchant ships that had also fallen into French hands made up the second category, while the third consisted of civilians. With the coming of peace in 1802, many English people had gone to France, either to travel or take up residence there. When war broke out again, some 10,000 were in the country and all were interned by the French. All three classes were given only small financial allowances by the French Government. While there were ways in which money could be obtained from England, many of the inmates were very badly off, especially since many were not imprisoned as such, but lodged in the various towns in which the depots were situated.

In the first instance, the Committee of the Patriotic Fund resolved to donate £500 towards 'the alleviation of the sufferings of prisoners of war' and that a committee of five be established at Verdun, which was the main depot holding the prisoners, in order to handle the monies. The Committee nominated Captain Jaheel Brenton, who had been captured in 1803 when his frigate was wrecked off Cherbourg, as one member and a Dr Alexander Allen another. They were to appoint the other three members.

This first grant and subsequent ones enabled the hospital at Verdun to be maintained and for schools to be set up for the children of the prisoners. John Robertson, a merchant skipper who had been shipwrecked off the French coast, noted that one of these schools, situated in the citadel at Arras, taught 'reading, writing, arithmetic, etc. and is upheld by the Patriotic Fund and at this time there is not less than 200 boys in it'. In addition, the Fund also provided each Army and Navy prisoner with a small additional financial allowance.

The merchant seamen were not provided for by the Fund, and in May 1806 some 220 masters of merchant vessels who were held in France addressed a petition to John Julius Angerstein for assistance. The Committee, however, rejected this on the grounds that merchant seamen were not directly involved in the defence on their country. Even so, Angerstein felt that something must be done to relieve their plight. He therefore initiated a special subscription, which would operate independently of the Patriotic Fund. By the end of July this had raised some £650.

The masters were still not happy, however. Because the French Government made a higher allowance to those who had skippered ships of 80 tons and above, the money raised by Lloyd's went only to those of smaller vessels. Each of these men was granted a Louis d'Or per month, which equated to one pound sterling. The masters of 80 tons and over vessels received 29 livres (£1 4s 2d per month) from the French, while the others were given only 14 sols (7d) every ten days. The former twice asked Captain Sir Thomas Lavie, who appears to have been made chairman of the Verdun Committee after being captured when his ship was wrecked off Ushant at the beginning of March 1807, to request Lloyd's to rethink their grants. Lavie's brother, Germain, was one of the original Committee members of the Patriotic Fund, which probably explains why Sir Thomas was made chairman. He had also previously been awarded a £100 sword for the capture of a French frigate. Even so, these connections did not cause any change of heart on the part of Lloyd's.

In January 1807 two prisoners, who had been exchanged, attended a Patriotic Fund Committee meeting. One was Captain Brenton, who had been exchanged for the nephew of one of Napoleon's marshals, André Massena. They were able to give the Committee first-hand accounts of conditions and how the Patriotic Fund monies were being spent. Their reports encouraged the Committee to continue to make annual grants. At the same time, the suffering inflicted among the dependants of those who fell or were badly wounded at Trafalgar also encouraged the Patriotic Fund to embark on other ways of bringing relief.

Chapter Four

NEW ENDEAVOURS AND INCREASING PRESSURES 1806–1814

The year 1806 saw the Patriotic Fund enter a new charitable field – education. The establishment concerned was the Royal Naval Asylum and the spur was the £77,000 that had been raised at the services of thanksgiving for the victory at Trafalgar.

In 1798 a Mr Thompson had founded a society called the British Endeavour with a view to establishing a place of education for the children of sailors along the same lines as the Military Asylum which had been established by the Duke of York for soldiers' children. He purchased a house in Paddington for this purpose, but while he was adept at raising money, he soon proved to be less capable of managing it, and was later sent to prison for fraud. The Duke of Sussex, who was one of the subscribers, was sent in to investigate the school's affairs, but had to resign due to failing health.

The Duke of Cumberland took over as president, and Horatio Nelson became one of its sponsors. The attention of George III was drawn to the school, and he 'declared his intention to make it a royal foundation for 1,000 children'. To this end, a Royal Warrant was issued on 25 July 1805 appointing 'Commissioners for the government of our Royal Naval Asylum, which it is Our Intention to establish at or near Greenwich'. The reason for the move was because the Paddington premises were limited to just 70 pupils. Money was needed to establish the asylum in its new location, and it was at this juncture that the Patriotic Fund became involved.

Independently, the Committee had begun to consider ways in which children of those who had fallen in defence of their country could be helped. A sub-committee was appointed for this purpose, and support for the Royal Naval Asylum appeared the perfect solution. After negotiations with the Commissioners, the sub-committee proposed that the sum of £40,000 be made available from the monies collected on the Day of Thanksgiving for Trafalgar. In return, the Commissioners agreed 'to maintain and educate such Children as may be nominated by the Committee for managing the Patriotic Fund, and as are within the rules of that Institution'.

Priority for places at the asylum was given to boys, the view being that 'it is most expedient that the Girls, except under particular circumstances, should remain under the care of their Mothers, with an annual allowance to defray the expence of clothing and educating that at day schools'. Each daughter would be granted £5 per annum until she reached the age of 14 and a local clergyman or 'some other person who shall be approved of by the Committee' would ensure that it was properly spent.

The Committee approved these recommendations at its meeting held on 22 July 1806 and agreed that applications from those living in England and Wales should be submitted to the Secretary of the Patriotic Fund at Lloyd's Coffee House, while the Secretaries of the Patriotic Funds in Edinburgh and Dublin would process applications from those living in Scotland and Ireland. Advertisements would be placed in the newspapers. The Committee also agreed that not just children of seamen who had been killed would be considered. The same help would be given to children whose fathers were on board HM ships 'in distant service' and whose mothers had died or were coping with large families. Families of seamen disabled in defence of the country were also included.

Rigorous proof that applications were genuine was required. Applicants had to enclose marriage and birth certificates, a doctor's certificate that the child or children were 'free from mental and bodily infirmity', and proof that the father had been killed in action or was serving afloat overseas. In the case of girls' annuities, a declaration was needed from a vicar or 'other person of respectability' that the girl 'shall be placed at a day school until in his opinion, she is sufficiently instructed in reading (writing, if possible) and plain needlework to furnish her with decent clothing and to pay the mother any surplus which may remain after providing for those objects'. The mothers themselves also had to undertake to send their daughters to school regularly and to ensure that they attended church on Sundays.

The money voted by the Patriotic Fund to the Royal Naval Asylum was handed over in the form of £61,000-worth of 3-per-cent Consols. The idea was that the interest paid all expenses incurred by the Committee's nominations at the school.

The Committee considered the first applications at the beginning of September 1806. Typical of them was that from Anne Ellis of Portsmouth, whose husband William had been killed on board HMS *Donegal* at Trafalgar. She applied on behalf of all four of her children – William (aged 9), Elizabeth (12), Louisa (6) and Harriet (3). The Committee granted William a nomination for the Royal Naval Asylum, 'dependent on the necessary testimonials', while £5 annuities were given to Elizabeth and Louisa. Harriet, however, was deemed too young, since the Committee considered that schooling was of no benefit to children under five. Her mother was invited to apply again on her behalf once she had reached this age.

The first Patriotic Fund nomination to enter the Royal Naval Asylum, one William Jones, was admitted on 10 November 1806 and by the end of the year he had been joined by two others. Jones, of whom little is known, would remain a pupil there for six years. Before the year was out, the Committee relaxed its rule on girls attending the asylum and also conceded that boys could be awarded the £5 annuity *in lieu* of being admitted. Members also made a snap inspection of its premises, which were still in Paddington, although shortly to move to Greenwich.

According to the minutes of the meeting held on 9 December: 'They found the Girls to be very keen, in comfortable attire and at their work; and the Boys in the School with the School Master, an intelligent young man.' He himself had been educated at the

asylum, they noted. The Committee also observed that the boys were able to earn some pocket money by spinning window sashes and twine.

The move of the asylum to Greenwich took place in November 1807. At this time there were 58 boys and girls in the school and they moved into the Queen's House. James I had originally initiated this in 1616 as a retreat for his queen, Anne of Denmark. She died three years later and building work was halted, but was resumed after ten years by Charles I for his bride, Henrietta Maria. It was now made over to the Royal Naval Asylum and, to enable the house to accommodate the 1,000 children envisaged by George III, two wings, connected by colonnades, were added. The plan was that the boys would occupy the two wings and the girls the house.

Thereafter there was a rapid expansion in numbers from 337 in 1808 to more than

800 by 1815. The Patriotic Fund nominations also rose from two in 1806 to nine in both 1807 and 1808, and 22 in 1809. From then on they averaged three per year.

Teaching and discipline for the boys were in the hands of the 'Quartermaster of Instruction' and his 'Sergeant Assistants', of whom there was one to every 50 pupils. There was no school bell. Instead, everything was done to the beat of the drum, which awoke them in the morning, marched them to meals and prayers, and summoned them to bed. For this purpose a naval drummer was employed. Education remained limited, with boys and girls leaving at the age of 14. They were, however, given some instruction 'to qualify them for duties of Seamen, or other stations in life'.

As the Royal Asylum was being established, the war against Napoleon continued. On 2 December 1805, the Emperor inflicted a defeat on a combined Austrian and russian force at Austerlitz. So decisive was it that Austria made peace. Prussia and Saxony, encouraged by Britain, now entered the war, but in October 1806 were utterly defeated at Jena-Auerstadt. Napoleon entered Berlin and Emperor Frederick William of Prussia fled to Russia. Determined to prevent the Russians from bolstering Prussia, Napoleon advanced into Poland. He won a victory at Eylau in February 1807 and then in the early summer inflicted a series of defeats on the Russians in what became known as the Friedland campaign. Both Czar Nicholas and Frederick William were forced to make peace. Trafalgar may have saved Britain from invasion, but it did not stop Napoleon from conquering continental Europe.

Yet, there were some glimmers of light. If Britain could not exert any influence on events in northern Europe, she could try to do so elsewhere. One of the first instances of this came early in 1806. On 6 February, Admiral Sir John Duckworth's squadron in the Caribbean attacked a french force based on five battleships off San Domingo and totally destroyed it. The Patriotic Fund awarded Duckworth a £400 vase and each of his captains a £100 vase or sword.

Then, in the summer of 1806 attention switched back to the Mediterranean. The British Force sent out in the spring of 1805 to cooperate with the Russians in northern Italy had been deployed to Sicily. In July 1806, its temporary commander, Sir John Stuart, used his own initiative to mount a raid on the Italian mainland. He met a french force at Maida and repulsed it with comparative ease, thus demonstrating that Napoleon's armies were not totally invincible and could be beaten. But other French forces then threatened Stuart and he was forced to withdraw back to Sicily. Nevertheless, when the news of Maida reached London at the beginning of September, Stuart was acclaimed a hero.

The Patriotic Fund voted him a £300 vase 'as a testimony of the high sense entertained by this Committee of his gallant conduct in that engagement, in which the pride of the presumptuous enemy was severely humbled, and the superiority of the British troops most gloriously proved'. Awards were also made to a number of wounded officers. They ranged from £200 for a severely wounded major to £25 each to one lieutenant and two ensigns. The Committee also agreed to make further awards once it had received full lists of killed and wounded.

This was not the only success that the Committee considered at this meeting held on 16 September 1806. It also had in front of it the latest edition of the *London Gazette*, which included despatches from General William Beresford and Commodore Sir Home Popham. The Committee already knew the latter, since it had had the pleasure of awarding him a £200 vase earlier in the year. This time the acknowledgement was for his part in the capture of the Cape of Good Hope from the Dutch in January. It had been achieved at the light cost of 16 soldiers killed, eight missing, and 199 wounded. The surrendered Dutch forces were given every courtesy and shipped back to Holland at British expense. The land force commander, Sir David Baird, was also awarded a vase, in his case to the value of £300, and financial awards to the wounded made on the same scales as those laid down for Trafalgar. Interestingly, two officers elected to receive vases to the value of £100 for their wounds instead of money. Six months later, Popham had further good news to tell. Again, this was the case of an officer on the spot operating on his own initiative.

Popham soon became bored in South Africa and persuaded General Baird to lend him the 71st Highlanders. He took them and 400 men borrowed from the Governor of St Helena across the South Atlantic and arrived off the River Plate in June 1806.

His original intention was to seize Montevideo, but he changed his mind and instead captured the richer prize of Buenos Ayres, capital of the Spanish colony of Argentina, on 2 July. Unfortunately, a few days later the local inhabitants rose and took the small British land force prisoner. In part, this was because of rage generated by the fact that the Commodore had seized one million dollars from the local treasury and sent the money back to England. Popham now blockaded the River Plate, but was unable to do more until he had received reinforcements.

The Patriotic Fund Committee was, however, in ignorance of the surrender when it considered the matter at its 16 September meeting. It was also likely influenced by the fact the Popham's gold dollars were now lodged in the Bank of England to the joy of the City. The Committee decided to award him and Beresford £200 vases for 'their gallant and disinterested conduct in this successful and important enterprise'. It also granted a disabled captain in the 71st Highlanders a £25 annuity for life and stated its intention to make further awards once it had the full casualty list.

Yet, there were indications at this same meeting that the Committee was beginning to feel the need to watch its purse strings. True, the Patriotic Fund was continuing to receive some donations. During 1806 monies came in from the colonies and from organisations and individuals at home. The City of Manchester, for instance, raised a total of nearly £6,000, much of it collected in 174 named ale-houses. The organisers originally wanted to disperse the money themselves, but, as the Committee had previously ruled in the case of the Durham subscription, they were persuaded to hand it over to the central fund.

Even so, the Army was becoming increasingly engaged in the war and casualties in land battles were significantly higher than those incurred at sea. Demands on the Fund were therefore on the increase. Probably with this in mind, the Committee decided that, in future, no more honorary awards would be made to Army officers above the rank of captain and that awards would only be made to relations of those killed and wounded if they could prove financial dependency on the sailor or soldier concerned.

As for Popham, when the true facts of the affair at Buenos Ayres came out, the Government was intensely angry. It summoned him back to England to account for departing the Cape of Good Hope without orders or leaving a single warship for its protection. He was court-martialled on board HMS *Gladiator* in Portsmouth harbour in March 1807 and after a five-day trial was found guilty, but received the very mild punishment of a reprimand.

A few days later, Popham visited Lloyd's Coffee House, where he was cheered by the Subscribers and made a speech. Not all, however, shared the general enthusiasm. *The Times* published a satirical report of the visit. It included a spoof of Popham's speech, which read in part: 'At Buenos Ayres, however, it was contrived, with no common management, to take a town, ship off all the dollars, and lose all the army. But, whatever may have been the fate of the brave men who composed the latter – whatever difficulties may attend, whatever blood may be shed in the recapture of the Colony, I have the honour to assure you that "Maldonado is safe".' Maldonado itself was a small village at the mouth of the River Plate, which was occupied by reinforcements sent out in autumn 1806.

The newspaper also published a letter from a Member of Lloyd's and signed 'An Old Subscriber'. He condemned those that claimed that Popham was a victim of 'ministerial animosity'. He went on: 'I wish, instead of wooing the applause of the Body who compose our Room, and inciting us by commending his conduct, to condemn a late decision, I could have witnessed him paying a respectful deference to the sentence of his Court-Martial. I wish I could have beheld him, as he ought to have done in the first, more particularly in this instance, making the voice of the Merchants, and opinions of the Underwriters on his conduct, subservient to the due authority of His Majesty's Councils.' But, as far as the City was concerned, 'Old Subscriber' and *The Times* were clearly in a minority, for the Corporation of London voted him a sword. The Admiralty, too, quickly forgave Popham and in July 1807 appointed him Captain of the Fleet for the second expedition against Copenhagen.

South America itself continued to prove an unhappy hunting ground for British arms. In the initial enthusiasm that was generated by Popham's capture of Buenos Ayres, the Government despatched further expeditions intent on wresting South America from Spain. Under General Sir Samuel Auchmuty, 3,000 men were sent to join the force at Maldonado on the River Plate with the aim of recapturing Buenos Ayres, while another 4,000 under Colonel Robert 'Black Bob' Craufurd embarked at Christmas 1806 on a very much more ambitious venture. It was to sail round the Horn, seize Valparaiso and then cross the Andes and link up with Auchmuty. A third, under Arthur Wellesley, was also formed to seize Mexico, but, in the event, did not sail. Auchmuty decided that his forces were too weak to retake Buenos Ayres and instead captured Montevideo in February 1807, earning himself and Admiral Stirling, the naval commander, £200 Patriotic Fund vases.

In reaction to the loss of Buenos Ayres, the Government now ordered Craufurd to join Auchmuty and sent out a more senior officer, John Whitelocke, to take overall command of the Plate Force and seize Buenos Ayres. After an exhausting approach march, he reached the city at the beginning of July 1807. But an over-complicated plan, involving no less than 13 separate columns simultaneously fighting their way in, came to grief in the narrow streets. Whitelocke was forced to sign an agreement with the Spanish agreeing to withdraw from the region. In this instance, there was no question of the Patriotic Fund making any honorary awards for this ignominious defeat, but again it gave financial help to those wounded and the families of the dead.

The Committee continued to meet every week in the Merchant Seamen's Office at the Royal Exchange, although on one occasion, in November 1806, it had to adjourn since only seven members were present as opposed to the nine needed to make a quorum. His Majesty's ships were continuing to cut out enemy vessels, resulting in further awards of swords to junior officers in charge of the boats. But this triggered complaints from officers of Royal Marines.

The incident that brought the matter to the boil was the capture of a privateer and the storming of a fort by the crew of HMS *Loire*, the second time that this ship had come to the attention of the Committee. Her captain, The Hon Frederick Maitland, one of the leading frigate captains, received a £100 sword from the Fund, and Lieutenant James Yeo a £50 vase and £50 sword. *Loire's* marine officer, Lieutenant Samuel Mallock, considered that he should also have received some recognition. Others supported him, including a major-general of Royal Marines and Lieutenant Yeo. One of the others, Captain Dashwood RM, wrote to the Patriotic Fund: 'From the nature of the service, they (Royal Marines officers) never can command a boat, consequently they cannot be placed in so conspicuous a situation as their rank and merit entitles them to. It is a well known fact, that the very idea of a Sword, however trifling its

value, spurs on the officer to deeds of the most heroic valour; and I believe it is pretty clearly ascertained that when officers lead, British Sailors and Soldiers are sure to follow.'

The Committee considered these letters at its meeting on 16 December 1806 and decided to award Mallock a £50 sword. Honour was therefore satisfied and the Committee ensured that in future it would not ignore His Majesty's Sea Soldiers. Thus, when boats of HMS *Galatea* successfully cut out the French corvette *Lynx* on 21 January 1807, the officer in charge of each boat and the officer commanding the marines were awarded Patriotic Fund swords.

In one case, an officer turned down the award of a vase in favour of something else. Commodore Sir Samuel Hood, another highly successful frigate captain, was awarded a £300 vase for a spectacular action off Rochefort in September 1806, when his squadron captured no less than four French frigates. During the course of the action, 'I received a severe wound in my right arm (since amputated, and doing well I hope), which obliged me to leave the deck'. Hood requested that the vase be converted to 'two or more of smaller size' which he intended to use as wine coolers. The Committee agreed to this and the two wine coolers that resulted are now in the possession of Lloyd's.

The Patriotic Fund also continued to make some awards to the lower deck for distinguished actions. The minutes of the Committee meeting held on 4 November 1806, contain the following: 'Read a letter from Captain George Collier of HMS *Minerva*, dated off Cape Finisterre, the 28th of July, recommending Peter Ward, Gunner's Mate and Coxswain of the barge, belonging to that ship, who, having boarded a Spanish Privateer, and while in the act of rendering assistance to one of the wounded prisoners lying on the deck, was treacherously fired at by him with a pistol,

which Ward wrested from his hand, threw it overboard, and persevered in his kind offices towards him.' Ward was awarded £20 'in testimony of the high sense in which the Committee entertain of his generous and humane conduct'. Certainly in one case, an officer made light of his wounds so as not to worry his family. Captain Atcheson Crozier of the Royal Marines was dangerously wounded during the successful storming of a French battery on Martinique in November 1803. He was awarded a £50 Patriotic Fund sword, but insisted on being marked as merely 'slightly wounded' on the casualty return. Sadly, Crozier eventually succumbed to his wounds, dying in 1807. The Committee was clearly moved by his subterfuge, since not only did it award his widow the sum of £100, but also an annuity of £25, which was, on her death, to be passed on in equal shares to her children – the son until he was 21 and the two daughters for life.

Occasionally, too, awards were returned to the Fund. The widow of Private Mark Scott of the 81st Regiment, who fell at Maida, was granted £40, but three weeks after the award was made, all but £5 were returned, no reason being given. In another case, a grant from the Patriotic Fund to a female relative of a man who had been killed resulted in her losing her allowance under the Poor Laws. The Committee was angered by this and resolved,

'That it is the opinion of this Committee that the relief which spontaneous patriotism has through this fund devoted to the relatives of those who may fall in the defence of the country, was never intended to supersede the assistance to which by the Poor Laws they might be entitled but to alleviate in some degree the loss of those for whom age and poverty had a natural claim, and that in the event of such parochial or township allowance being discontinued, in consequence of a vote from this fund, its operation would be to relieve the parish or Township, and not the object for whose benefit such money was intended.'

In other words, Patriotic Fund grants were not merely given out to assist the recipients financially, but also in the hope that they would provide some consolation for the loss of a loved one. A copy of this resolution was sent to the administrators of the Poor Laws in Manchester, where the woman lived.

Even though Britain still stood on her own in Europe as the only nation still determined to resist Napoleon, her strategy became increasingly one of attack rather than defence. The operations in South America may have proved abortive, as did others. At the end of 1806, Admiral Sir John Duckworth, in an effort to relieve the French pressure on Russia, led a squadron through the Dardanelles and into the Sea of Marmora. It remained there, while the British ambassador tried to bully the Turkish Sultan into joining the allies. Simultaneously, a small British Force was landed in Egypt, but soon found itself blockaded in Alexandria. The Turks resisted the British demands and Duckworth was forced to withdraw, incurring casualties from the Turkish batteries as he passed back through the Dardanelles. These abortive operations resulted in additional calls on the Patriotic Fund, with £4,285 alone being paid out to Duckworth's wounded.

Better success attended the second assault on the Danish capital Copenhagen. This was prompted by French pressure on Denmark and fears that the Danish fleet would fall into Napoleon's hands. On 16 August 1807, troops under Arthur Wellesley, supported by Lord Gambier with 17 ships of the line, landed on the Danish coast and advanced on Copenhagen. The Danes, although militarily very weak, refused to surrender, and the city had to be subjected to three days' bombardment before white flags appeared. The whole Danish fleet, consisting of 15 battleships and 30 smaller vessels was then removed out of harm's way. However, in this instance no honorary awards were made from the Patriotic Fund,

although monies were paid out to the wounded and dependants of those killed.

In March 1808, the Committee decided to revise its scale of gratuities paid to the wounded. These were now placed in four rather than three categories – loss of limb, disabled, severely wounded, and slightly wounded. The new rates were to be as follows:

	Loss of Limb	Disabled	Severely	Slightly
2nd class	£150-200	£100-150	£80-100	£40-50
3rd class	£80–100	£75	£40–50	£20–30
4th class	Up to £80	- not specified -	not specified -	
5th class	£20–40	£15–30	£10–20	£5–10

As far as the Army was concerned, the Committee rated captains in the second class, lieutenants and ensigns in the third, sergeants in the fourth, and junior ranks in the fifth.

Widows of seamen were to be paid between £20 and £40, those of soldiers between £20 and £30, and parents of deceased seamen between £15 and £20. Parents of soldiers and other relations of both soldiers and sailors would only be granted sums, which were unspecified, if they could prove 'loss of support or assistancy'. The Committee gave no reason why soldiers' relations should receive slightly less favourable treatment than those of seamen, but it is likely that this reflected the fact that the Army's pension system was more efficient than that of the Royal Navy.

At this same meeting, the Committee also considered a proposal from the Reverend George Burder of Hatton Garden to the Bishop of London that the Patriotic Fund provide Bibles or Testaments for use by seamen's messes on board ship. This was rejected as 'not within the meaning of the Patriotic Fund Institution'.

The year 1808 also witnessed a more significant British military expedition overseas. With Spanish permission, French

forces had invaded and overrun Portugal at the end of the previous year. Then, on the pretext of wanting to protect the Spanish coastline from invasion, a French army of 100,000 men marched into Spain. King Charles IV was forced to renounce his throne and Napoleon made his brother Joseph, King of Spain. This brought about a revolt and the British Government began to send arms to both Portugal and Spain. It also began to organise a military force to be sent to the Iberian Peninsula.

The high point of the revolt came in July 1808 when a Spanish Force defeated 20,000 French troops at Baylen. On 1 August the British force, under Arthur Wellesley, landed north of Lisbon and three weeks later defeated the French army in Portugal at Vimiero. A simultaneous uprising in Lisbon itself sealed the French fate, but by now Wellesley had been superseded by two more senior generals, who allowed the French troops in Portugal to be taken back to France in British ships.

There was an understandable outcry at home and Wellesley and his superiors were recalled. Their place was taken by Sir John Moore, who advanced into Spain. By this time the Spanish revolt had been all but crushed and the French forces in the country were able to concentrate against Moore. Heavily outnumbered, he was forced to withdraw. A grim winter retreat through the mountains, with the French forever snapping at their heels, culminated in the British troops reaching the northwest Spanish port of Corunna, where the Navy was waiting to evacuate them. But Moore's men first had to repulse the French to buy time for the evacuation. This they did, but Moore himself fell in the hour of victory.

The Committee of the Patriotic Fund was soon busy dealing with the large number of cases arising from the campaign. Not least was an immediate grant of £500 to assist the exhausted and emaciated survivors when they were landed at Plymouth.

Among the recommendations was one from Lt Col Edward Hull, commanding the 2nd Battalion of the 43rd Regiment. He drew the Committee's attention to one of his former sergeants, William Newman. During the retreat to Corunna, he was ordered to collect stragglers and sick and bring them along to rejoin the main body. Marauding French cavalry caused panic, but Newman managed to gather some 100 out of the 400 to 500 men he had with him and form them into a rearguard. Over a distance of some four miles he repeatedly halted and turned on the French, repulsing them on each occasion. Eventually, he caught up with British cavalry, who drove the enemy's cavalry off.

Newman's conduct was brought to the attention of the divisional commander and he was rewarded with a commission in the 1st West India Regiment. His former commanding officer ended his letter: 'As however, there must necessarily be a great expense in fitting himself out, and preparing for his Voyage, I beg to recommend him in the strongest manner to your favourable notice.' The Committee took due note and awarded Ensign Newman £50 'in testimony of the high sense which the Committee entertain of his gallant & meritorious conduct'.

Another recommendation came from Major Charles Napier, one of three famous soldier brothers, and concerned Mrs Jane Russell, the wife of one of his private soldiers in the 50th Regiment. The Army allowed six wives per company to accompany their husbands on campaign and they made themselves very useful as nurses, washerwomen, and in other tasks. Mrs Russell was awarded £15 by the Fund for her care of the sick and wounded during the retreat.

The majority of the cases arising from the first campaign in Portugal and Spain did not come before the Committee until summer 1809, but by this time another British Force had landed in Portugal. Again, it was Wellesley who led it, but this time it was

there to stay. As they had done the previous year, the British troops soon cleared Portugal of the French and advanced once more into Spain. On 24 July, Wellesley fought the Battle of Talavera against the combined forces of Marshal Victor and Joseph Buonaparte. Although he succeeded in forcing the French to withdraw to Madrid, his Spanish allies deserted him and he suffered heavy casualties. It was clear that Spain was not to be liberated from the French yoke at one blow.

Back in London, the news of the victory at Talavera was greeted with joy, but the Committee of the Patriotic Fund was concerned over the high casualty bill. The balance in the Fund stood at some £93,000, but the Committee members calculated that it was likely that they might have to pay out some £130,000 to meet the Talavera claims. With Sir Francis Baring in the chair, the Committee met on 24 August to consider the problem. Clearly economies had to be made and it was a question of confirming the Patriotic Fund's priorities. A resolution was put forward that, 'in view of the enlarged scale upon which the Military Operations of the Country are now carrying on', it was necessary to revise the original resolutions on which the Fund was based.

Henceforth, it was proposed, it should concentrate on the relief of the families of those killed in action, help for those suffering from loss of limbs or whose wounds were so disabling as to prevent them from continuing in the service of their country and, finally, continued support for the aged and sick prisoners of war in France, their hospitals and schools. What this meant was an end to honorary awards and those to men whose wounds were not permanently incapacitating.

Joseph Marryat, who made the main speech in support of the resolution, said of the latter: 'The man who receives a wound from which he suffers only temporary pain, but

no permanent injury or inconvenience, is in some degree compensated for that pain, by bearing an honourable scar, received in the service of his country, and surely he will not repine at no gratuity being voted to him from this fund, when he knows that he can only receive it by depriving the widow and orphans of some of his comrades of their means of support. The saving made by this regulation would amount to nearly one half of the present total expenditure of this institution.' As for the honorary awards, Marryat accepted that the saving was 'trifling', since a total of only £16,400 had been spent on them to date. Even so, 'claims of merit alone ought to yield to claims of merit and distress combined.'

The Committee passed the resolution unanimously. At the same time, it instituted a fresh subscription in honour of Talavera and this raised a total of £32,317.

The last honorary awards made by the Patriotic Fund concerned an operation to destroy the French Atlantic fleet. It had managed to break out of Brest and was anchored in the Basque Roads, close to the border with Spain and protected by powerful shore batteries. On 11 April 1809, two vessels loaded with explosives and 19 fireships, under the command of Captain Lord Thomas Cochrane, attacked the French anchorage. They forced the French ships to cut their cables and in the ensuing panic all but two ran aground. Unfortunately, the main British fleet under Lord Gambier hesitated to take advantage of this and only four of the French ships were destroyed before they could be refloated. Nevertheless, Cochrane, who had already been awarded a Patriotic Fund £100 sword for cutting out a French corvette in the River Gironde, received the thanks of parliament and two officers, Captain James Wooldridge and Lieutenant Nicholas Clements, both of HMS *Mediator*, were awarded swords for their gallantry when commanding fireships during the action.

Although they had not strictly been killed in action, the Committee did grant gratuities to their dependants. While honorary awards had ceased, permission was given to a few officers to use gratuities granted to them to have swords made to the same pattern as the Patriotic Fund swords, together with a suitable inscription. One, Captain Brenton of HMS *Spartan*, even managed to have the cost of his sword passed through the account that Mr Teed, who made the swords, had with the Fund.

In Europe, Austria, encouraged by events in Spain, had turned against the French early in 1809. Austrian armies invaded Bavaria and Italy that April, but were soon thrown back and in May the French once more entered Vienna. The climax came in July when Napoleon broke the Austrians at Wagram, forcing them to sue for peace for the third time. Britain was again on her own, with Wellington (he had been ennobled after Talavera) holding on to the one toehold that the British had on the continent of Europe. With uncertain allies, Wellington had to proceed cautiously and between 1809 and 1811 he remained largely on the defensive, anchoring his operations on fortifications which he constructed in Portugal, the Lines of Torres Vedras.

This is not to say that battles were not fought. The French were bent on invading Portugal and time and again Wellington had to block them. Battles like Bussaco, Fuentes d'Onoro, and Albhuera were among his victories, but they also resulted in an increasing number of cases to be dealt with by the Patriotic Fund. The minutes of the Committee meetings were filled with

Sadly, the meeting held on 24 August 1809 was the last Sir Francis Baring attended. On 11 September he died, much mourned by the Lloyd's community. His contribution to the setting up and running of the Patriotic Fund had been immense and those who had benefited from it owed much to him. The chairmanship now passed into the equally capable hands of John Julius Angerstein and the work of the Committee continued unabated.

At sea, the blockade of French ports continued. In the West Indies the British and Spanish went over to the offensive, gradually seizing all the French colonies there. British ships were also operating in the North Sea and Baltic. At a meeting held in October 1810, the Committee considered a sad letter from Captain James Newman of HMS *Hero*. It enclosed a list of 26 officers and men of his crew, who had been wrecked on the coast of Mecklenburg in the Baltic while hunting for small Danish privateering boats. Local soldiers had forced them to put back to sea in a violent storm and all were drowned.

grants, the recipients being listed by regiment. The foreign corps fighting with Wellington's army – units like the King's German Legion and Chasseurs Britanniques – were also included. Thus, five soldiers of the King's German Legion each received £5 for wounds received at Talavera. There was also a steady trickle of naval casualties.

The demands on the Fund meant that gratuities were often less than laid down in 1808. At its meeting on 8 October 1811 the Committee granted £15 to a seaman who had lost a leg, and £30 to a corporal of marines who had lost both legs, significantly below the £20–£40 that they might have expected to receive. Likewise, the widow of a captain of the 88th Regiment (the Connaught Rangers) who fell at Fuentes d'Onoro was given a £20 annuity, when she might previously have been granted a £25 one. It was also noticeable that the Committee meetings were now very much longer in duration because of the number of claims on the Fund, and from 1811 a quorum was reduced to five members, presumably because less of them could spare the time.

The Committee's concerns were aggravated at the beginning of 1812 when the Fund's bank, Messrs Bolderos & Co, failed. Luckily, there was a policy in force that only sufficient monies would be held in the bank account to satisfy imminent demands on the Fund. Even so, nearly £5,000 was in the account at the time and its loss was one that the Committee could have done without. At the time that the crash happened, both Angerstein and Thomson Bonar were out of London, but the third Trustee, Robert Shedden, whose family was beginning a lengthy connection with the Fund, acted with commendable speed. He gave Secretary John Welsford a letter of credit on his own bank to cover grants which were being currently processed, and then drew up a list of possible replacement banks, selecting those who had contributed to the Fund when it was originally set up. The Committee considered these at an extraordinary meeting held on 7 January and selected Shedden's own bank, Messrs Smith, Payne & Smiths. As for the money lost with Bolderos, the Fund did, over the course of the next 45 years, recoup some 60 per cent of it.

This extraordinary meeting also looked at the case of a seaman of HMS *Little Bell* who was disabled by wounds received in action against the American frigate *Constitution* off the US coast the previous May. Relations with the United States had been deteriorating. The Americans were resentful that the Royal Navy continually impressed the crews of their ships, while the British were increasingly concerned over US designs on Canada. In April 1812 matters degenerated into all-out war, which was characterised by a number of epic frigate versus frigate actions at sea and full blown campaigns on land. The seaman himself received £10 and was to be the first of many claims from this conflict.

The Patriotic Fund did enjoy some relief, however. It had continued to provide grants for the prisoners in France and during the years 1805–11 it had paid out a total of £27,200. A national subscription to assist the prisoners was initiated early in 1812 and succeeded in raising a total of £74,000. The Committee therefore decided in March that, because of the reduced state

of the Fund and the ever increasing demands on it, it should cease providing financial support to the Verdun Committee.

In Europe, 1812 was to prove the turning point of the long war against revolutionary France and Napoleon. His invasion of Russia in June proved to be a disaster. Although he reached Moscow, Napoleon found himself at the end of over-extended lines of communication, which came under evergreater Russian threat. Faced with the approaching Russian winter, he had little option but to withdraw. The result was little short of catastrophic. Suffering from cold and hunger, and constantly harried by the Russians, the much-vaunted *Grande Armée* was reduced to a mere 10,000 effectives by the time it had struggled into the relative security of Prussia in December.

In Spain, too, Wellington went over to the attack. His first task was to seize the two frontier fortresses of Cuidad Rodrigo and Badajoz. He successfully stormed the former on 19 January, but the siege of Badajoz proved a much grimmer affair. It took a month's close investment to reduce it and the British losses were heavy.

The members of the Committee discussed Badajoz at their meeting of 25 April, just 18 days after the fortress surrendered. They had in front them casualty lists to the tune of 5,557 killed and 16,536 wounded, and the Fund stood at £80,770. There was no doubt that it would be severely stretched to meet the fresh demands on it and the Committee decided that the only answer was to raise another subscription. To set it in motion, the Committee proposed to the Subscribers of Lloyd's that they donate £5,000 in 3-per-cent Consols. The Badajoz Subscription raised nearly £21,700, two-thirds of that for Talavera, but sufficient to tide the Fund over for the time being.

Meanwhile, Wellington was not resting on his laurels. After a week's manoeuvring he brought the army of Marshal Marmont to battle at Salamanca on 22 July. Three weeks later, Wellington liberated Madrid. Once more British church bells rang in celebration, but again the Patriotic Fund Committee's joy was tempered by the inevitable additional pressures on the Fund.

Since Talavera, the Committee had handed out over £30,000 to seamen and naval dependants and nearly £91,500 to the Army. The Talavera and Badajoz subscriptions had covered only just over one quarter of the total and normal subscriptions to the Fund had declined from an average of nearly £45,000 per year during the period 1805–9 to barely £10,000. As long ago as February 1807, it had begun to sell stocks, but the Committee obviously had no wish to make too many inroads into its capital, since the interest from this provided the bedrock for the Fund's operations in the future. Consequently, on 1 September 1812 the Committee resolved to establish a Salamanca subscription. The announcement in the press read:

'The signal and glorious Victory, on the plains of Salamanca, achieved through the transcendent military skill and conduct of the Marquess of Wellington, by the intrepid gallantry and firmness of the brave officers and men under his command, has been duly estimated by the admiring and grateful people of this Realm, whose exalting satisfaction has recently been expressed in the most general and conspicuous manifestations of their pride & joy. The Committee of the Patriotic Fund feel it their duty, on this great occasion, to call on their Countrymen to enable them to continue the relief so well earned, and so highly deserved by brave men who have fallen or have been disabled in this noble conflict, for themselves, or the widows, orphans & relatives who depended on them for their support.'

The notice went on to make the point that the Fund had already provided assistance to 13,254 cases, 'including the deserving & heroic sufferers' of Salamanca and that it still had 'a large number of the most meritorious claims on its accustomed assistance'. It then appealed to 'the generous sympathy of all ranks of a discerning people, sensible of the blessings of Security from the hostile and vindictive aims of its powerful enemy and rival, the British Seaman and Soldier may still confidently trust, that those who are dear to him while living, shall, in the event of his falling in the sacred cause, find friends in a grateful and generous Country; and that he who may be disabled in its defence, shall not be neglected by those, whom he has bravely defended.' Within two weeks the subscription stood at nearly £40,000, including £10,000 worth of Consols donated by Lloyd's. The officers of the 7th Hussars each contributed a week's pay and the NCOs and men two days' pay. The war went on. Wellington was unable to capitalise on his success at Salamanca and failed to capture the fortress of Burgos. With winter now upon him, he fell back and went into winter quarters near Cuidad Rodrigo. In northern Europe, Napoleon's allies were deserting him. In January 1813 there was a revolt in Prussia that forced Napoleon's troops to withdraw to the Elbe. Prussia, Russia, Sweden and Britain then

formed a new coalition. Austria joined the alliance the following August and it gradually forced Napoleon on to the defensive. The year culminated in the three-day Battle of Leipzig in October, after which the French withdrew across the Rhine. In Spain, Wellington won a resounding victory over Joseph Buonaparte at Vittoria in June and then drove the French back across the frontier. The Committee continued its work and one seemingly unusual case was considered in February 1813. It was brought by General Sir Thomas Picton, one of Wellington's leading commanders and who was later killed at Waterloo. It concerned Captain Benjamin Williamson. He was a retired officer on half pay, who had borrowed £2,500 in order to obtain commissions for his two sons. This reflected the fact that the British Army of the day relied on the purchase system in which officers brought their commissions for money, the concept being that it maintained their motivation through giving them an investment in the Army. Each step in rank up to and including Lieutenant Colonel had to be purchased, the officer selling on his previous commission. Those who had won battlefield commissions, like Edward Newman of the 43rd Regiment, who had so distinguished himself during the retreat to Corunna, or had received promotion in the field also gained financially in that their commissions were

also saleable commodities. In this case, Captain Williamson hoped that his sons would win promotion and enable him to repay the debt. Alas, both were killed in Spain in 1812, at Cuidad Rodrigo and Burgos respectively, and their father was left in an embarrassing predicament.

The Committee presumably took the view that he had some financial dependence on his sons and awarded Captain Williams £300. Three years later it considered a similar case, brought by the brother of Lt Col Crawford, who fell in 1813. In this case, the brother had loaned the colonel the money to purchase his commission and the brother now found himself in financial straits, especially since he had four children. In this instance, he received £400 from the Fund.

What appeared, at the time, to be the final act of the war now took place. The Austrians, Prussians and Russians invaded France from the east, while Wellington, having pushed his way through the Pyrenees, threatened from the south. At the end of March 1814, allied troops entered Paris. Napoleon realised that the game was up and abdicated. He was banished to the island of Elba and the French monarchy was restored. After more than 20 years of war, peace had finally returned to Europe. But it was not to last.

Chapter Five

WATERLOO TO THE CRIMEA 1815 - 1856

Throughout the remainder of 1814, the Patriotic Fund continued to pay out monies to the wounded and dependants of the dead of the late campaigns. But the war with America continued throughout the year and many of Wellington's Peninsular veterans were shipped across the Atlantic to reinforce the British forces. The Treaty of Ghent to end the war was signed on Christmas Eve, but news of it did not reach North America until February 1815, by which time the British had suffered their worst defeat of the war at the Battle of New Orleans a month earlier. And there was worse in Europe.

On 1 March 1815, Napoleon landed at Cannes on the French Riviera, having given the allied ships the slip and escaped from Elba. As he progressed northwards towards Paris, Frenchmen, many of them veterans, flocked to his standard. Within just a few weeks he had raised a field army of 200,000 men, with a further 300,000 recruits in training. The allies declared him an outlaw and began to organise themselves once more for war. A British force under Wellington was sent to Belgium and Dutch troops came under his command. By 1 June his troops were concentrated on the French border, with a Prussian Army under Marshal Bluecher close by.

The Patriotic Fund Committee reviewed the situation at its meeting held on 23 May. Since its inception, the Fund had received a grand total of £543,450 in subscriptions and interest on its investments. It had paid out well over

£480,000, including gratuities to 11,230 wounded, 2,352 widows, 3,126 children and 1,345 other dependent relations. This was no mean contribution to the welfare of Britain's Armed forces, but there was no room for complacency.

The Committee had in front of it figures which represented the total British casualty bill since May 1803. The Army had suffered 12,272 killed and 54,354 wounded, while the Navy's share was 1,971 killed and 6,327 wounded. The implication was that the Committee could still expect a significant number of applications for assistance in the future, irrespective of the fact that further bloodshed was now inevitable. Clearly, it was going to continue to have to watch its finances.

The campaign was, however, to be short, but bloody. Napoleon left Paris on 11 June, secretly concentrated his army and seized Charleroi. He then began to advance against the allied armies. Wellington met one wing of the French Army at Quartre à Bras on 16 June, but managed to keep it at bay. Napoleon, with the main body, attacked Bluecher at Ligny and forced him to withdraw. Wellington now retired towards Brussels and took up position at Waterloo, which he had previously reconnoitred.

On 18 June, Napoleon attacked him and a day of 'hard pounding' followed. The French battered themselves in vain against the allied line. The final attempt to break through was made by the cream of Napoleon's army, the Old Guard. When that failed, Wellington began to counterattack. At this moment, the Prussians appeared and continued the pursuit into the night. Four days later, Napoleon abdicated once more and made his way to Rochefort, where he surrendered to the British. The frigate HMS *Bellorophon* then took him to the remote South Atlantic island of St Helena, which he would never leave.

The first news of the victory at Waterloo reached England on the evening of 20 June, when an agent of the banker Nathan Rothschild arrived from Ostend with a Dutch newspaper, which gave a somewhat garbled account of the battle. This was in the hands of the Cabinet by the following morning, but few believed it. That evening, however, one of Wellington's *aides de camp*, Henry Percy, arrived in London with Wellington's despatch and two captured French eagles. The next day, the 22nd, the news spread like wild fire across the country, but the joy was tinged with sadness and shock at the size of the casualty list. Within just a few days, meetings were held in towns and cities throughout Britain to raise money for the wounded and dependants of the dead. The monies collected were then transferred to a general fund, which became known as the Waterloo Subscription. This raised nearly half a million pounds.

The Committee of the Patriotic Fund would have been, understandably, relieved that a potential additional burden was to be shouldered elsewhere, although some of its members were involved in the Waterloo Subscription. John Julius Angerstein presided at some of its committee meetings, and John Welsford was secretary to the City branch of the fund, to which Lloyd's contributed £10,000-worth of Consols. As far as the Patriotic Fund was concerned, the only comment on the Waterloo Subscription appears in the minutes of the committee meeting held on 12 July 1815.

The members decided to make a public announcement. This cited the statistics reviewed during the 23 May meeting and made the point that the Fund had only £63,000 available and was, apart from other claimants, still awaiting some 6,000 appeals from the war with America. In the light of this, 'the Committee observe with great satisfaction, the renewed and extended expression of the public admiration and Gratitude towards the disabled of the intrepid and brave soldiers, Combatants on the glorious 18th of June at Waterloo and towards the Relations of those who fell on that memorable day.'

During the next few years the Committee remained busy. Indeed, over the period 1816–23 it gave help to 783 men who had lost limbs, 2,396 with disabling wounds, 297 officers, 620 widows and 109 children. It continued, too, to make nominations to the Royal Naval Asylum. The Committee was also careful to obey its own rules when considering gratuities. In May 1816, a request was made on behalf of a widow of an officer of the 79th Regiment, who had been wounded on three separate occasions during the Peninsular War and had then been killed at Waterloo. It is not clear whether the widow had already claimed off the Waterloo Fund for her husband's death, but as far as his wounds were concerned, the Committee considered that he should have claimed for them at the time and, in any event, grants given to the wounded were to aid their recovery and not to help support their dependants.

A similar application was made from the widow of a naval captain who had died off West Africa. The address on the letter was Marshalsea Prison, Southwark and so presumably she was an inmate, possibly for debt. Her husband had also been wounded on three occasions and she had four children. She asked if she might have the money that would have been granted to her husband if he had claimed off the Fund for his wounds. Again, the Committee turned down the request.

In another case, a seaman on board a merchant vessel had lost both arms and an eye when one of the ship's guns discharged unexpectedly during the firing of a salute. The Committee expressed its regrets, but stated that the tragedy fell outside the Patriotic Fund rules.

The year 1816 witnessed an additional demand on the Fund. For some years the Barbary States (Algiers, Tripoli, Tunis and Morocco) had plagued the western Mediterranean with piracy, some directed at obtaining European slaves. During the Napoleonic Wars, the combatant nations found it politic to pay protection money on their ships, although the Americans did wage wars against Tripoli and, later,

Algiers. Now, with Napoleon finally vanquished and outrages continuing, the British decided to take action. In August an Anglo-Dutch fleet under Lord Exmouth bombarded the port of Algiers and destroyed the Bey's fleet.

One of the claims subsequently made on the Fund was from Rachel Mackenzie, the wife of a seaman on board HMS *Superb* and who had been present at the bombardment. She declared that her health had suffered as a result of the bombardment and *Superb's* captain backed this up. The Committee granted her £10 in compensation.

In autumn 1820, the Committee received a letter from another lady, Mrs Louisa Cooke, whose late husband had been killed at Trafalgar while in command of HMS *Bellorophon*. She had, of course, received a presentation of plate from the Fund and had declined any financial assistance. Now she wrote to say that she had been disappointed in her hopes that the government might provide her with adequate financial support and considered 'her prospects in life much changed by circumstances unforeseen and unavoidable'. The Committee declined to give her aid on the grounds of the current state of the Fund.

It was doubtless with this in mind that in 1821 the Committee decided to revise the rules regarding those annuities granted to widows which were allowed to be passed on to their children on their death. Henceforth, it was decided, the offspring would only be allowed to enjoy the annuity until they reached the age of 21, 'except under special circumstances to be decided by the Committee'.

The same year also brought about a significant change to the Royal Naval Asylum. In January 1821 the Committee received a letter from Lord Melville at the Admiralty, which administered the school, giving details of a plan to merge it with the School of Greenwich Hospital

for economic reasons. By this time, the Patriotic Fund had nominated 100 boys and 134 girls to the asylum and there were currently ten of these boys and nine of the girls attending the school. The Royal Hospital School itself had been founded by William and Mary as an adjunct to the Royal Naval Hospital, its purpose 'the Maintenance and Education of the Children of Seamen happening to be slaine or disabled in such Sea Service and Also for the further reliefe and Encouragement of Seamen and Improvement of Navigation'. It was, however, not until 1712 that the funds were available to set up the school, with the boys being dressed in the same uniform as the naval in-pensioners. They did not begin to receive a proper education until three years later, when ten of the boys were permitted to attend lessons at the nearby Weston Academy.

This was a private school for the gentry of Greenwich and was founded by Thomas Weston. Among its alumni were James Wolfe, the hero of the capture of Quebec in 1759, and Admiral John Jarvis Earl St Vincent, one of the great naval commanders of the Napoleonic Wars. The fee-paying pupils were given a comprehensive education in the arts and sciences, but the boys from the Royal Hospital received only sufficient to prepare themselves for a career at sea, especially in the Merchant Service. Indeed, the object was to fit them for the rank of Master's Mate, which required skill in navigation.

By 1759 there were well over 100 Royal Hospital boys attending the academy and accommodation became too cramped. The boys were therefore provided with their own school building and the link with Weston's ended. The education was then broadened to a degree, but the emphasis remained on seamanship in accordance with the original 1694 charter. In 1783 the boys moved out of the Royal Hospital itself to a new purpose-built structure known as Stuart's Building after its architect. When the

Royal Naval Asylum moved to Greenwich, the two schools had remained entirely separate, even though they were geographically virtually neighbours. There was little love lost among the boys of the institutions, and fights were not infrequent. Now it was intended to merge the two, but the Patriotic Fund Committee felt that it should take legal advice before giving its assent. In particular, the lawyers were asked to look at the proposal in the light of an Act of Parliament that had been enacted in July 1817. This formally empowered the Commissioners of the Royal Naval Asylum to make any use they saw fit of the interest generated by the stock lodged by the Fund for the school as long as it was for the 'benevolent purposes' of the asylum. The lawyers saw no conflict of interest and the Committee approved the merger. On 31 January, King George IV duly signed a Royal Warrant commanding 'that the school of Greenwich Hospital is now transferred to the Naval Asylum and the funds of the two schools are incorporated'.

Initially, the former Hospital School was known as the Upper School of the Royal Asylum, but in 1825 the title 'Asylum' was dropped and the institution became known as the Upper and Lower Schools of the Royal Hospital. At the time of the merger, however, the differences between the two were stark. The Lower School had 600 boys and 200 girls and was essentially a trade school, the boys automatically joining the Navy as seamen on leaving, while the girls generally went into service, with those not finding a post being sent to 'their friends'. Entry was between the ages of 9–12 and 14 was the compulsory leaving age. Education *per se* was a low priority, the boys having just one master, with a boy taken from the Upper School as his assistant.

In contrast, the 200 boys of the Upper School had three qualified teachers and were being trained to be officers in the Merchant Service. They were accepted between the ages of 11 and 12. A boy

from the Lower School could, however, graduate to the Upper School on the recommendation of one of the directors of the school. Patriotic Fund nominations continued, however, to be restricted to the Lower School.

In 1824 the Admiralty began to take a closer interest in the Upper School. Some 70 boys a year were graduating from it, but there were insufficient berths in merchant ships for all of them. Consequently, it issued a circular encouraging Upper School boys to apply to be appointed Volunteers 2nd Class and Master's Assistants. They would be supplied with uniform and kit and were guaranteed at least seven years' service in the Royal Navy.

Three years later, the Duke of Clarence (the future William IV, 'the Sailor King') proposed that the Upper School be increased to 400 pupils at the expense of the Lower School, the additional 200 boys being Admiralty nominations. The directors of the hospital resisted this on the grounds that it was still difficult to place all the boys leaving the Upper School and there was a large number of applications for admission to the Lower School from poverty-stricken families. A compromise was therefore reached, and the Admiralty was allowed 100 nominations. Then, in 1829, through an Act of Parliament, the Lords Commissioners of the Admiralty took over total control of the school. Five commissioners would look after its finances and a governor its discipline. The Committee of the Patriotic Fund appears not to have had strong views one way or the other over these changes, but it maintained a strong line over its right to make nominations to the Lower School. In June 1826, the members went so far as to forward a resolution to the directors of Greenwich Hospital decrying delays in accepting pupils put forward by the Fund and 'strenuously' asserting

'their privilege that all children recommended by them shall be immediately admitted into the Royal Naval Asylum according to the original agreement, without being subject to the delay of waiting for vacancies.'

With regard to its main work, during the year ending 28 February 1823, the Committee gave assistance to 30 limbless, 413 other disabling wounds, and 27 widows and orphans. One of the saddest cases it had to deal with was that of the wife of a Lieutenant Craig Royal Marines. He had been voted a £25 annuity in 1804 on account of his wounds, but was now suffering from 'mental derangement' and was confined to a Dublin lunatic asylum. Mrs Grey asked leave to draw on his annuity when it became due and the Committee granted permission for her to do so provided that her bill was accompanied by signed certificates from the physician and surgeon, and witnessed by a magistrate, that her husband was still alive at the time.

The members realised, however, that they could not carry on dealing with these cases *ad infinitum* and in May 1823 they decided that they would accept no more retrospective cases after 20 July 1824, the 21st anniversary of the Patriotic Fund's foundation. Some of the cases that now came in went back many years. In September 1823, a private in the Royal Artillery was awarded £15 for wounds received at Buenos Ayres in August 1806. The following May, Captain H H Dobbie of the Royal Navy received £250 for a serious musket-ball wound to the chest while commanding a squadron of three brigs in operations against 'piratical vessels' in the West Indies in 1803.

Another turning point in the history of the Patriotic Fund was also marked in 1823. In January, John Julius Angerstein passed away at the ripe old age of 87.

He was the last of the original trustees, Thomson Bonar having been murdered in May 1813, together with his wife, by a footman whom they had recently taken into service and who had beaten them over the head with a poker.

Angerstein himself, with his previous experience of raising subscriptions, had been a tower of strength from the outset. His standing in the City and his wide circle of friends had been of immeasurable value and he had worked tirelessly for the Fund. Although he did not physically chair Committee meetings after March 1815, he remained chairman until his death and maintained an active interest in the Fund. Among his other interests, Angerstein built up of fine collection of paintings, which later formed the foundation of the collection at the National Gallery, London.

Robert Shedden, whose quick thinking had done much to limit the damage done by the Bolderos Bank crash, succeeded him as chairman. This was the beginning of the 'Shedden era' of the Fund's history, since Robert was succeeded by his son George and he, in turn, by his son William George.

Given the continued high number of retrospective applications, the Committee decided that May to extend the deadline by one year, to 20 July 1825. Yet, even as late as February of that year it considered no less than 66 cases at one meeting. When the gates did finally close, the Committee resolved that the remaining monies be invested to provide:

'a foundation for a subscription in the event of a future war, thereby perpetuating the benefits of an Institution so honourable in its commencement to the Merchants and Underwriters at Lloyd's and so zealously and unanimously supported by every class and every description of persons throughout the United Kingdom; a subscription which in its amount stands pre-eminent of all other subscriptions in this country.'

But the gates barring retrospective claims were not entirely bolted. As late as December 1831 an extraordinary meeting was called to consider the case of Captain Sir W H Mulcaster, who had previously been awarded a £50 Patriotic Fund sword for his part in cutting out five Spanish vessels in Finisterre Bay in June 1806. Mulcaster was continuing to suffer from a wound to the hip received during the capture of Fort Oswego on Lake Ontario from the Americans in May 1814. It had 'ever since remained open and that abscesses with exfoliation of bone frequently take place'. This and another wound received many years before, during the action of the Glorious First of June 1794, had entitled him to a government pension of £300 per year, but the later wound was considered by the Royal College of Surgeons to be the equivalent of the loss of a limb. Captain Mulcaster stated that he had not realised, until too late, that he could have applied to the Fund for a gratuity on these grounds. The Committee took pity on him and made an award of £300.

During this period, British forces were involved in only one significant action. In January 1822 the Greeks, who had been long under Turkish rule, declared their independence and the country rose in revolt. It took the Turks, aided by the Egyptians, three and a half years to restore their hold and during this time a number of Europeans, including Lord Byron, went out to fight alongside the Greeks. Indeed, so popular did their cause become that in July 1827 the governments of Britain, France and Russia felt forced to issue a joint demand for the Egyptians to withdraw and for the Turks to enter into negotiations.

When this was ignored, an allied fleet under Sir Edward Codrington was organised and destroyed the Turko-Egyptian fleet in Navarino harbour.

It was this action, more than any other, which enabled Greece to finally gain her independence through the Treaty of London of May 1832. There had been British naval casualties during the battle, but the Patriotic Fund Committee decided that it could not offer assistance, since the Battle of Navarino did not come under the terms of the original charter in that it had nothing to do with the direct defence of British interests.

Throughout the first 25 years of its existence, the Committee continued to meet at Lloyd's, although in 1813 it did acquire its own administrative office, since the Old Committee Room, from which it had been operating, had too many other demands on it. The office was situated at 45 Lothbury, which stood on the other side of the Bank of England from the Royal Exchange. This was not totally satisfactory, especially since the majority of the Fund's mail went to the Royal Exchange. However, in 1828 the Fund managed to obtain offices under the same roof as Lloyd's, at No 8 Royal Exchange Gallery which it rented off the City of London and the Mercers Company at 50 guineas per annum.

With no more retrospective cases to consider, apart from a very few exceptions, and the country not involved in any wars, the Fund was enjoying a quiet time. But, on the evening of 10 January 1838 the Royal Exchange caught fire. The cause was believed to be an overheated stove in Lloyd's rooms. The firefighters had difficulty in gaining access to the building and, because it was a very cold night, they had a problem with freezing water. Not until midday on the following day was the fire considered to be under control, but by then the Royal Exchange had been reduced to a ruin. It was a disaster, not just for the Patriotic Fund, but for Lloyd's as a whole.

Lloyd's itself managed to find alternate accommodation at South Sea Hall, on the corner of Threadneedle Street and Throgmorton, and was installed there within a week. Luckily, thanks to the initiative of one of the Subscribers, who happened to pass the Royal Exchange while it was burning, some of the key records were saved.

The Patriotic Fund, too, was grateful to John Lines, formerly Assistant Secretary to the Fund, who was appointed Secretary after John Welsford's death in 1828. On the morning of 11 January, with the help of the Superintendent of the Fire Brigade, he managed to gain access to his badly damaged office and rescue some of the books and papers, although fire and water had ruined much of the material. Crucial were the Minute Books, which were held in a safe. The safe itself was found intact, but the intense heat had damaged some of books. The current Minute Book (Volume 16) was in the worst state and John Lines had to copy its contents into a new book, as he also did for Volumes 14 and 15, which covered the period August 1820 to April 1836. The other 13 volumes survived intact.

Lines had also kept some personal papers in the office, all of which were lost. They included two mortgage deeds, leases, and three life policies. In compensation and for the extra work involved in copying the damaged Minute Books, the Committee awarded him the sum of £250, which equated to a year's salary.

There was no room for the Fund's office in South Sea Hall, and so the Committee found accommodation on the first floor of 37 Old Broad Street, but there was no suitable room for Committee meetings. Instead, these were held in the private room of Charles Harford, himself a Committee member, at Harford & Rivaz, 62 Old Broad Street.

Soon after the Fund was settled into its new offices, a growing problem at the Royal Hospital School began to come to the Committee's attention. The girls' part of the school in the Queen's House was situated between the two boys' schools. While they were officially not allowed to mix with the boys, it was inevitable that clandestine liaisons would take place. They also could not be prevented from meeting when going to and returning to their homes, many of which were in ports. 'These journeys,' the authorities noted disapprovingly, 'they perform in straw wagons or steam vessels, 20 or 30 together without any control and passing often many nights together on the road.' In an effort to improve discipline, the Board decided in summer 1834 to appoint two monitors from among the girls about to leave and to retain them until they reached the age of 17. They would be provided with £5 per annum as wages, 'victualled and clothed as other girls, with the exception of allowing them a cloak, gowns and bonnets similar to those supplied to the Nurses of the Hospital'.

The experiment was not a success. The monitors resented the fact that their undergarments seldom fitted since they were made for children rather than for girls fast reaching maturity. They were not given rooms of their own and, living cheek by jowl with the girls, were unable to exert much influence over them. In desperation, the Captain Superintendent of the school wrote to the Admiralty in November 1839 proposing that the girls' part of the school be dissolved.

The upshot was that the Admiralty launched an enquiry. Its recommendations were sweeping. The girls' school should be discontinued and the curriculum of both boys' schools remodelled. Additional staff should be appointed to both the Upper and Lower Schools, and an inspector appointed by the Admiralty

was to make half-yearly visits. The recommendations were accepted and by April 1841 all the girls had left, with the exception of one orphan who was placed in an apprenticeship with a straw-bonnet maker in Greenwich. The others were granted £12 per annum, provided they attended a local school. This would terminate at the age of 14, when, if they had been allowed to stay, the girls would have left the Royal Hospital School.

This had implications for the Patriotic Fund, since it had been nominating girls, as well as boys, for the school. After negotiations with the Admiralty, it was agreed that the Fund would be allowed to nominate an average of an additional five boys a year, who were to be sons of merchant seamen, for the Upper School.

By the time this matter had been resolved, the Patriotic Fund had begun to deal with a fresh crop of cases resulting from wars about the Empire and elsewhere. In the Near East, the Ottoman Empire, faced with a revolt in Egypt, appeared to be crumbling and the major European powers, except for France, decided that there was a need to prop it up to conserve the balance of power. A British fleet cooperated with the Turks by bombarding and occupying Beirut and Acre in autumn 1840.

The Committee agreed that victims of the bombardments should be entitled to assistance from the Fund. It accepted that it

was acting on a 'broader basis' than previously and was now prepared to assist in any conflict in which British forces were involved, apart from those in India, which remained under the control of the Honourable East India Company. During the next few years, the Committee considered cases from the First China War (1839–42), otherwise known as the Opium War, the First Maori War in New Zealand, naval operations with the French to quell piracy in Madagascar, and, also in conjunction with the French, the bombardment of Argentinian batteries in the River Plate in November 1845 aimed at preventing Argentina from annexing neighbouring Uruguay.

There was only one British casualty in this last operation, William Collier, cook on board HMS *Dolphin*, who was killed. His mother received £15 from the Patriotic Fund in compensation. But, even though the rules of the Patriotic Fund had been relaxed, the Committee was not prepared to make every conflict eligible. In June 1847 a Royal Marines Colour Sergeant of HMS *Columbine* was killed during an action against pirates off the coast of Borneo. The Committee declined to make a grant to his widow, probably on the grounds that the territory was not a British possession and the north coast was a private fiefdom under James Brooke, the Rajah of Sarawak.

At this time, Lloyd's as a whole instituted an honorary award. For some years it had

been making cash awards to recognise the saving of life at sea. The system was, however, not very satisfactory in that the Committee of Lloyd's could not approve these awards on its own. The general approval of the Subscribers was needed, and this could only be obtained at a general meeting, which were held only twice a year, or by calling a special general meeting.

In 1836, after some debate, the Committee was empowered to prepare medals 'for extraordinary exertions in saving lives from Shipwreck'. However, it was three years before specimens were approved. A Lloyd's Medal for Saving Life at Sea was awarded in gold, silver or bronze and the first man to be decorated with it was Captain Martin Walsh. He was master of the schooner *Alicia* and he received the silver medal for rescuing passengers and crew from the stricken American sailing ship *Glasgow* in the Irish Sea in February 1837, although it was not until May 1839 that he received his medal. The Lloyd's Medal continues to be awarded to this day and is highly prized by its recipients.

If the 1840s were characterised by far-flung colonial conflicts and skirmishes, including wars against the Afghans and Sikhs in India, the next decade witnessed a major war involving European powers. The focus was again the ailing Ottoman Empire and the balance of power in Europe. The pretext was squabbles among the clergy in

Turkish-occupied Jerusalem over who should have jurisdiction over the Holy Places. Czar Nicholas I, as protector of the Orthodox Church, saw this as an opportunity to dominate Turkey and secure access to the Mediterranean from the Black Sea. In July 1853, Russian troops occupied Rumania. Alarmed, the British and French sent ships to Constantinople to bolster the Turks. Encouraged by this, the Turks declared war on Russia at the beginning of October 1853. After the Russians destroyed a Turkish naval squadron at Sinope at the end of November, the Anglo-French fleet moved into the Black Sea and demanded that the Russians withdraw. They ignored this, and after a Russian army invaded Bulgaria in March 1854, Britain and France declared war. Both hastily organised expeditionary forces, which were despatched to Varna on Bulgaria's Black Sea coast.

The British troops left for the Black Sea amid a wave of popular euphoria. But there was immediate concern over the families they left behind. A number of local schemes were hastily enacted and this quickly led to the formation of a national organisation, The Central Association for the Aid of Wives and Families of Soldiers Ordered to the East. Its main objective was to find the wives work, so as to encourage them to become independent. Taking their children off their hands would make it easier for them to do this. Care of the families of those

serving overseas was, of course, well outside the remit of the Patriotic Fund and its Committee did not review the situation until the end of May, when it decided that it was premature to take any action over raising a new subscription.

By this time, the British Force under Lord Raglan had just arrived at Varna and was joined by the French a few days later. Hopes of early action against the invading Russians in Bulgaria were dashed, since they not only halted their advance but also withdrew from Silistra, which they had placed under siege. Efforts to make peace were frustrated, though, by the Russian refusal to undertake to leave the Ottoman Empire alone. Meanwhile, the allied forces at Varna were subjected to a cholera epidemic, which resulted in 10,000 fatalities without a single shot fired in anger. In view of the inactivity, the Patriotic Fund Committee decided at their meeting on 28 July that there was still no point in taking any positive action while the lack of significant military and naval operations continued.

The allies now decided on a change of strategy. They identified Sevastapol, the major Russian naval base in the Black Sea, as the primary threat to the Ottoman Empire and decided to move their forces from Varna to the Crimea in order to seize the port. The landings, which were unopposed by the Russians, took place during 13–18 September, and the following day the advance towards Sevastapol began.

On 20 September, the allies encountered the Russians for the first time. They were holding the high ground dominating the south bank of the River Alma. After a grim fight, the British forced them back, suffering 2,000 casualties in the process. The allies then closed on Sevastapol and by early October had invested it. The Russians made two attempts – Balaclava on 25 October and Inkerman on 5 November – to break the siege, which dragged on through the winter. Conditions were miserable, especially for the British, whose inadequate and hopelessly inefficient supply system broke down under the strain.

On 17 October 1854, the Patriotic Fund Committee had in front of it the casualty list from the Battle of the Alma. It was also aware of an announcement in the *London Gazette*, four days earlier, that a Patriotic Fund had been established by Royal Charter for the 'succouring, educating and relieving those, who, by the loss of their husbands and partners in battle, or by death on active service in the present war, are unable to maintain or support themselves'. This created a dilemma. Not only had this new subscription taken the same name, but it also had much the same aims as the Fund established by members of Lloyd's 50 years earlier.

The Committee members were the very opposite of petty-minded and certainly had no wish to challenge the Royal Commission appointed to manage the Royal Patriotic Fund. But the Patriotic Fund was by then relying almost entirely on the £1,600 annual interest on its investments and it would need to raise a new subscription to enable it to assist those serving in the Crimea and their families in the same way as it had in the past. But to raise a new subscription might be interpreted by the general public as an attempt to rival the Royal Patriotic Fund and so the members

dismissed it as inappropriate. Instead, they decided to approach the Secretary of the Royal Commission and ask of him how they might conveniently dovetail the operations of what now became known as Lloyd's Patriotic Fund with those of the Royal Patriotic Fund. It was not until December that they received confirmation that the Royal Patriotic Fund would not cover either those disabled from wounds or dependants other than widows and orphans. Consequently, at its meeting held on 16 January 1855, the Committee agreed that it would use the Fund to support these two classes and an announcement to this effect was published in the Press.

Before it could make any grants to the disabled, the Committee obtained the agreement of the Admiralty and War Office that they would furnish details of the pension that each man was being paid so that the degree to which he could support himself could be established. Not until July 1855 were the first Crimean awards made by Lloyd's Patriotic Fund. Dependent parents of those killed received £10 each, while a guardsman received the same amount for a lost leg, and three others £5 each for unspecified disabling wounds.

Another who received help was the mother of Captain Louis Nolan, the officer who carried the misleading order from Lord Raglan to Lord Cardigan which resulted in the charge of the Light Brigade at Balaclava and who was killed in the charge. Mrs Nolan had lost her husband and two sons in quick succession and apparent investments in the West Indies had proved disastrous, leaving her to subsist on a government pension of a mere £50 per year. The Committee granted her the sum of £50. However, the application for an annuity for the mother of an officer killed at Inkerman was rejected, since the Committee was no longer making this type of award.

In December 1855, the Committee, as it had done on previous occasions, decided to draw up a scale of awards for disabled soldiers, placing them in three categories:

	Sergeant	Corporal	Private
Totally disabled ie. missing two limbs or blinded	£20–£25	£15–£20	£12 10s to £15
Unable to earn but otherwise needs no assistance	£15	£12 10s	£10
Capable of supporting himself but not fit to soldier	£10 to £12 10s	£7 10s to £10	£5 to £7 10s

These sums were less than they had been 50 years earlier, but pensions had much improved. For instance, a totally disabled sergeant received 2s 6d to 3s per diem, while a private discharged as medically unfit on account of his wounds, but capable of earning his own living, could expect between 8d and 1s.

By the time this scale of grants had been drawn up, the Crimean War was virtually at an end. Sevastapol had finally fallen to the allies in September after the French successfully stormed the Malakoff Redoubt. This marked the end of the fighting in the Crimea, although largely naval operations designed to bottle up the Russian Northern Fleet in the Baltic continued. On 1 February 1856, the equivalent of an armistice was signed in Vienna and the peace was ratified the following month in Paris.

As had happened after Waterloo, there was no reduction in the number of the cases applying for help from Lloyd's Patriotic Fund or, for that matter, from the Royal Patriotic Fund, which like that of Lloyd's was now established as a permanent charity.

Chapter Six

THE HEIGHT OF EMPIRE
1856-1914

Lloyd's Patriotic Fund assisted some 2,600 cases arising out of the Crimean War. Among them was the widowed mother of Private Thomas Corcoran of the 17th Lancers, who fell in the Charge of the Light Brigade. Even though Corcoran was not the best behaved of soldiers, having been twice court-martialled, the Fund granted her £5 in May 1859.

More distinguished was the first Victoria Cross (VC) winner to come to the Committee's attention. This was Captain of the Foretop Thomas Reeves of HMS *Albion*, who was part of a shore party manning naval guns in the siege works around Sevastapol. The citation for his award stated: 'At the Battle of Inkerman, when the right Lancaster Battery was attacked and many of the soldiers wounded, Seaman Reeves, with two others [also awarded VCs] and two others who were killed during the action, mounted the defence work banquette and, under withering attack from the enemy, kept up a rapid, repulsing fire. Their muskets were re-loaded for them by the wounded soldiers under the parapet and eventually the enemy fell back and gave no more trouble.'

Reeves later, in September 1855, suffered a disabling wound to his right arm and the Fund awarded him £10 for this, with an additional £5 in recognition of his bravery. He received his Cross from Queen Victoria herself at the very first investiture for Britain's highest award for gallantry, held in Hyde Park on 26 July 1856. Reeves was discharged from the Navy on the grounds of 'age and infirmity' when aged 32 and Lloyd's Patriotic Fund made its grant five

months later. Sadly, he then contracted tuberculosis and died within two years.

It would seem that he had no close relations, since he was buried in a mass paupers' grave at Portsea Island General Cemetery. When Portsmouth's continental ferry terminal was expanded in the 1970s, it engulfed the cemetery and Reeves' body could not be traced. The name of this gallant sailor might have been totally forgotten, but, thanks largely to the efforts of the Greenwich Royal Naval Association Victoria Cross Memorial Fund, a memorial to Thomas Reeves was erected in one of the Ferry Port arrival halls and unveiled by the Lord Lieutenant of Hampshire in November 1999.

In the immediate aftermath of the Crimean War, Lloyd's Patriotic Fund moved its premises once more, obtaining offices on the third floor of County Chambers at 14 Cornhill, renting them from the County Fire Office. It held its first meeting there on 30 June 1857. Charles Dickens Junior listed the Fund at this address under 'Philanthropic Societies' in his *Dickens's Dictionary of London* (1879). The entry appeared between those for the Ladies' Dressmaking and Embroidery Association and School of Dress Making and the London Anti-Vivisection Society. Dickens noted that there were no subscriptions to the Fund and none solicited and that its object was 'to grant assistance to such soldiers, seamen, and marines, as well as officers, or their widows, orphans, or dependent relatives, as in the opinion of the trustees shall be fitting objects for such aid, having special regard to sufferings and losses arising during services in action'.

In 1875 the capital stock of the Fund was placed in the hands of the Charity Commissioners and the Committee members were retitled Trustees. They continued to be busy, not just considering Crimean War cases, but those from other wars both before and since. These ranged from the Second China War, which arose from the Taiping rebellion and culminated in the storming of the Taku Forts in August 1860, to the Royal Navy's involvement in helping to crush an uprising on Haiti in 1865.

In January 1873 the Committee finally changed its policy over British forces serving in India. In the aftermath of the Indian Mutiny, the powers of the Honourable East India Company were gradually transferred to the Crown and it ceased to exist in 1873. In consequence, the Patriotic Fund Committee decided that members of the Armed Services in India would now be eligible for assistance, unless they were serving under native princes.

One early case concerned a Royal Artillery sergeant who was seriously wounded by 'a fanatic Musselman in Secunderabad', and was awarded £12 10s. In 1876, annuities were reintroduced and one of the first, for £25, was awarded to the widow of a subaltern in the 87th Regiment who had died of sunstroke in India.

November 1872 marked the end of the Shedden era in the history of Lloyd's Patriotic Fund, when William George submitted his resignation as chairman on account of ill health. His successor, William Saunders, had originally served in the East India Company's army as an engineer officer, before he joined his future father-in-law as a Lloyd's Underwriter. He had become a Patriotic Fund Committee member in 1849, but was principally known for his deep knowledge of flora and fauna, having been for many years a Fellow of the Zoological Society and Vice-President of the Royal Horticultural Society.

Saunders' tenure was unfortunately short. Within a year, his underwriting business had collapsed and he was forced to file for bankruptcy. He felt that he had no option but to resign the chairmanship. Charles Wigram, grandson of one of the original 1803 Committee members, succeeded him. He would steer the Fund through to the next century. As for Saunders, he obtained his discharge from bankruptcy in 1876 and played a valuable role as the Fund's representative trustee of the Royal British Female Orphan Asylum. Saunders' new appointment reflected the fact that the Fund had significantly enlarged its educational interests beyond the Royal Hospital School during the past 30 years. In May 1844, the Patriotic Fund had granted £8,000 to the Royal Naval School at New Cross. This was for the sons of naval officers and the Patriotic Fund money was to be used to 'board and educate, in perpetuity, on the Committee's nomination, Twelve Boys free of expense always, being the sons of Naval and Marine Officers eligible by the rules of the Royal Navy [sic] School to be received'.

Four nominations were made each year to bring the total up to 12. The Fund also helped the school in other ways during the next few years, providing £500 in 1852 for the building of a chapel, £20 in 1859 towards a swimming pool, and £100 in 1877 to help cover additional expenses incurred during an outbreak of scarlet fever.

Then, in 1864, the Fund made a grant of £5,250 to the Royal School for Daughters of Officers of the Army at Bath to cover five nominations in perpetuity. This was followed in 1879 by a similar grant, for £3,000, to the naval equivalent of the Royal School Bath – the Royal Naval Female School, Richmond. In this case, the grant covered two nominations. The school had applied to the Fund earlier for assistance, but at the time (1849), it felt unable to help.

The Fund did not, however, concentrate only on the officer class. It made a number of grants, including one in 1868 of more than £14,000 for 30 nominations to the Royal British Female Orphan Asylum, otherwise known as the Royal United Service Home for Girls, at Devonport. This had been established in 1839 and, according to *White's Devonshire Directory* of 1850, it housed some 60 girls, the daughters of sailors, soldiers and poor civilians.

In 1876, the Fund made a grant of £500 to the Royal Seamen and Marines Orphan School at Portsmouth for the nominations of ten girls, with the Fund paying £20

per annum towards the fees of each. Finally, 1,000 guineas was given for two nominations from orphans of the members of the 24th Regiment killed by the Zulus at Isandlwana in 1879 to the Soldiers' Daughters Home at Hampstead. Lloyd's Patriotic Fund also contributed to the national Zulu War Widows and Orphans Relief Fund.

Throughout this time the Fund continued to nominate pupils for the Royal Hospital School, the average number of these boys at the school being 40. In 1872, the Admiralty decreed that all boys leaving the school should enter the Royal Navy, unless found unfit, in which case they were bound for the Merchant Service. But openings for the Navy were becoming limited. This was especially after 1863, when the ranks of Master and Master's Mate were replaced by navigation lieutenant and sub-lieutenant, and candidates were drawn from the Navy's cadet school HMS *Britannia* and not from the Royal Hospital School. In addition, academic subjects were sacrificed for trade training, which made it difficult for the boys to attain commissioned rank. Worse, the trades themselves hardly fitted boys for the Navy. Indeed, shoemaking, shirt-making, tailoring and laundering gave the school the appearance of an East End sweatshop.

Another problem was domestic in nature. It was decided that the cost of each boy should be reduced from £30 to £18 per annum and, in consequence, the quantity and quality of the food suffered. The upshot

of this was that the fitness of the boys declined until nearly 40 per cent were unable to pass the Navy's entry medical. In 1881 the Admiralty set up a commission of inquiry, which investigated every aspect of the school. It found that over 80 per cent of the boys had been treated in hospital in the course of a single year and that their overall health was worse than in any other educational institution in London. They were only allowed 20 minutes for each meal and much of the food served was uneatable. The boys also wore the same uniform – thin Navy serge - in summer and winter. No evidence survives of what the Trustees of Lloyd's Patriotic Fund had to say about this, but given their philanthropic attitude, they were doubtless very concerned.

Wide-ranging reforms were introduced to make the boys more fitted for careers in

the modern Royal Navy. Money, however, remained a problem and both the Royal Hospital School and the Royal Naval School, which moved from New Cross to Eltham in 1889, approached the Fund's Trustees in the 1890s over the fact that their nominations could no longer be supported by the interest accruing from the sums that they had donated.

In the case of the Royal Hospital School, matters began to come to a head in 1894, when a Lloyd's Patriotic Fund nomination failed the medical which every boy had to undergo before entering the school. G J Lambert, the Director of the Royal Hospital at the Admiralty, wrote to the Secretary of the Fund to complain, pointing out that, in any event, the boy's father had been a Trinity House pilot and had never served in the Navy and so was ineligible for

admission to an orphanage at the expense of Greenwich Hospital funds. He reminded the Trustees that the 1817 Act stipulated that their nominations had to be 'within the rules of the Institution'. He also cited an 1883 Act under which some of the regulations of the Royal Hospital School had been changed.

The Trustees appear to have accepted this, although, of course, they did have the right to nominate the sons of merchant seamen. Two years later, however, the director lodged a more serious complaint, namely that the Trustees were making more nominations than could be maintained at the school. He pointed out that the interest from the original £40,000 was sufficient only to support 54 nominations, but that there were now 91 at the school.

The problem was that there was not a laid down ceiling for the number of nominations that the Trustees could make, as Charles Wigram pointed out in his reply. Nevertheless, the Trustees agreed to impose a limit of 65 nominations being present at the school at any one time. To this end, at the beginning of 1899, they put a temporary freeze on nominations. In 1898, the Royal Naval School made a similar complaint, stating that it was losing £450 per annum on the 12 nominations at the school and asked that the Trustees reduce these to six, which appears to have been done.

The main work of the Fund continued, increased by a succession of colonial wars. During 1879–81 a second war was waged against the Afghans and there were numerous campaigns on the northwest frontier of India, as well as one in Burma. Apart from the Zulu War, there was also a disastrous campaign against the Boers during 1880–81. In West Africa there were a series of campaigns against the Ashanti tribe. From 1882 the focus switched to Egypt and Sudan. A revolt in Egypt resulted in the death of Europeans. To crush it, British and French naval squadrons bombarded Alexandria and then a British Force under Sir Garnet Wolseley defeated the rebels at Tel-el-Kebir. A year later, in 1883, a figure called Mohammed Ahmed declared himself the Mahdi, or prophet, and set Sudan aflame. Not until 1898, when Kitchener finally defeated him at Omdurman, was peace restored to the region.

The Trustees remained wedded to the policy of giving grants to the wounded and dependants other than the children of those who had been killed. There were, however, exceptions. In April 1881, the Fund gave a grant of £20 to the son of a deceased officer to enable him to outfit himself for the Royal Military College Sandhurst. And there were also one or two other links to the Fund's early days.

In 1879 the Trustees granted the sum of £12 10s to 103-year-old David Bloomfield. He had been a sergeant in the 32nd Regiment and had been wounded at Vimiero, Wellington's first significant victory of the Peninsular War in 1808, and had fought in six subsequent major battles, being awarded an additional 6d per day on his pension for rescuing the regimental colour at Salamanca after the ensign carrying it had been killed.

A more curious case came to the Trustees' attention in 1897. A Member of Parliament instigated a fund to assist a woman who was over 80 and whose mother, the wife of a Royal Engineer, had taken refuge in the Forest of Soignies with her baby daughter while the Battle of Waterloo was being fought. The Trustees made a contribution to this fund to honour the only living woman who had been present at Wellington's crowning victory.

By this time, the Trustees were conscious that there had recently been a considerable increase in the number of Service charities. The Royal Patriotic Fund was continuing to support widows and orphans, and throughout the 1860s and 1870s was assisting some 3,700 widows of soldiers and sailors and 5,000 children. It had also established its own schools for boys and for girls. There were also a number of public subscriptions raised for the Afghan War, the Zulu War, and in the aftermath of Gordon's death at Khartoum in 1885.

That year also saw the founding of the Soldiers' and Sailors' Families Association (SSFA). The force behind this new charity was Colonel James Gildea, who had been involved with a number of charitable Service funds. In the wake of Gordon's death, another expeditionary force was despatched to Egypt and Gildea was concerned over the families that it, and those already serving in the country, had left behind. Consequently, he set up

committees around the country to identify Service families suffering from financial problems and to give them advice and support to encourage them to provide for themselves. The local committees helped the wives to obtain work and found places for their children in schools. They also made grants in the event of sickness or loss of employment, but these were of a temporary nature only, with no annuities being paid.

The instant success of SSFA was revealed by the statistics embracing its first five years in operation. Excluding help in finding employment, the association helped nearly 1,400 wives and more than 4,200 children. In addition, it provided succour for almost 750 other dependent relatives of soldiers, sailors and marines.

Furthermore, at least in the Army, the 1880s witnessed an increasing number of regimental associations designed to assist former members who had fallen on hard times. The torch which had been lit by Lloyd's almost a century earlier was steadily multiplying. Now, at the turn of a new century, Lloyd's Patriotic Fund was about to face a new challenge that would require close cooperation with these new charities.

In South Africa, relations between the British and the Boers, the descendants of the Dutch who originally started settling there from the 17th century, had been steadily deteriorating since the discovery of gold in the Transvaal in 1886. The province was under autonomous Boer rule, as was neighbouring Orange Free State, and they resented the influx of foreigners, most of them British, who arrived to make their fortunes. In 1895 there was an abortive attempt to incite an uprising in the Transvaal, which became known as the Jameson Raid. Thereafter matters deteriorated still further and, after a Boer ultimatum for the British troops guarding mining interests in the Transvaal was ignored, the Boers declared war in October 1899.

With the worsening situation, the Trustees had been discussing what action they should take in the event of war. Almost hours before it did break out, they had agreed the draft of an announcement to be published in the media and to be sent to the commanding officers of all regiments and ships. It stressed that Lloyd's Patriotic Fund was the oldest Service charity, having no connection with the Royal Patriotic Fund, and that its object was 'the relief of Soldiers, Sailors, their Widows, Orphans or Dependent Relatives, sufferers by War'. The announcement also made it clear that the Fund had raised no public subscription since the Napoleonic Wars and that since 1854 it had assisted in 4,500 cases. It was also supporting 126 pupils at various schools. Its capital now stood at only £75,000, bringing in £2,300 annual income, which was insufficient to give assistance to new cases that war in the Transvaal would inevitably bring.

To increase the Fund's standing, the Trustees also considered forming a council of patrons, with perhaps the Prince of Wales or Duke of York at its head, and consisting of distinguished soldiers and sailors. They also considered holding a public meeting in the Mansion House. But, as the Boers laid siege to Mafeking and Kimberley, the Fund found itself pre-empted, as it had been in 1854 at the outset of the Crimean War.

At their meeting held on 24 October, the Trustees heard that the Duke of Cambridge had appealed to the Lord of Mayor of London to initiate his own fund, which he called the Mansion House Fund and was 'for the benefit of the Widows, Orphans and other Dependants of those who may lose their lives by wounds or disease in the war operations in South Africa'. This put paid to any ideas of a Lloyd's Patriotic Fund meeting in the Mansion House. However, the Lord Mayor decided that some of the money raised by his fund should be handled by Lloyd's Patriotic Fund to assist soldiers 'disabled by wounds (for their benefit after they leave the service)'. This fitted in well with a change of policy over wounded agreed by the Trustees earlier in the year.

Charles Wigram had expressed his concern that the small grants for wounds the Fund was able to make 'leaves the recipient in no better position than before, whilst in many cases there is reason to fear that it is spent immediately and practically wasted'. Rather, he proposed that the grants should be under some supervision to ensure that they were for 'the permanent benefit of the recipient'. The sort of expense he had in mind was payment of the entrance fee to the Corps of Commissionaires, an organisation which had been set up in 1859 specifically to find suitable employment for ex-servicemen and policemen, the purchase of an artificial limb, or covering the costs of a stay in a convalescent home.

The Trustees concurred with the chairman's view and this was to be the policy of Lloyd's Patriotic Fund towards the wounded of the South African War. There was, however, recognition that they would need to liaise closely with other charities to ensure that duplication of effort was kept to a minimum, especially since new ones had sprung up.

One of these was the Soldiers' and Sailors' Help Society (later renamed the forces Help Society). It established a number of convalescent homes to assist the recovery of seriously wounded men. The Lord Mayor proposed that Lloyd's Patriotic Fund should allocate money from its 'Transvaal War Fund' to support these homes, but the Trustees initially declined to do so on the grounds that they wanted to concentrate on disabled men after they had been discharged from the Services. Even so, they agreed to work in conjunction with the society and within a month undertook to the pay expenses of men permanently disabled from wounds suffered in South Africa and who were in its homes. The Duke of Abercorn started his Sick and Wounded Officers Surgical Medical Aid Society and asked for help, but the Trustees declined to assist disabled officers although they subsequently relented.

In May 1900 the Trustees received a request from the manager of the Absent Minded Beggar Relief Corps for assistance to men on sick leave. The origins of this strangely named organisation lay with the proprietor of the *Daily Mail*, Alfred Harmsworth (later Lord Northcliffe). Like other national newspapers, he used his publication to raise a fund for the troops in South Africa. To publicise it, he commissioned a special poem from Rudyard Kipling. Its opening lines read:

When you've shouted 'Rule Britannia', when you've sung 'God Save the Queen',

When you've finished killing Kruger with your mouth,

Will you kindly drop a shilling in my little tambourine

For a gentleman in khaki ordered South?

He's an absent-minded beggar, and his weaknesses are great −

But we and Paul [Kruger] must take him as we find him −

He is out on active service, wiping something off a slate

And he's left a lot of little things behind him!

As usual, Kipling summed up the mood of the country. Men were volunteering in their droves for South Africa, especially as the news grew ever grimmer, particularly after 'Black Week' in December 1899, when the Boers were victorious in three separate battles. The poem went on to remind readers of the loved ones that the 'absent-minded beggar' had left behind him and the danger that many of them would become destitute. It ended:

So we'll help the homes that Tommy left behind him!

Cook's home − Duke's home − home of a millionaire,

(Fifty thousand horse and foot going to Table Bay!)

Each of 'em doing his country's work

(and what have you got to spare?)

Pass the hat for your credit's sake, and pay − pay − pay!

Sir Arthur Sullivan put the poem to music and it became an instant hit in the music halls. The fund itself eventually reached a total of £250,000, enabling it not only to aid the wounded and their families and send out medical supplies and comforts to the forces in South Africa, but also to run its own convalescent home. Lloyd's Patriotic Fund worked closely with the Absent-Minded Beggar Relief Corps. One example of their mutual cooperation was that when members of the Relief Corps boarded the hospital ships arriving from South Africa, they handed out application forms for assistance from Lloyd's Patriotic Fund, explaining how it could help those who had been disabled.

There was still a very real danger of the various charities tripping over one another in their efforts and, in order to help, HRH The Prince of Wales chaired a meeting in February 1900 to establish a national organisation to coordinate the work of the major funds. Lloyd's Patriotic Fund sent a representative and he was given a seat on the national committee that resulted from this initial meeting.

The 'South African Fund', as that portion of the Lloyd's Patriotic Fund handed over by the Lord Mayor's Mansion House appeal was finally to be called, reached a total of nearly £100,000 by the beginning of April 1900. At the same time, the Trustees were still dealing with cases from previous conflicts; for instance, at their meeting of 1 March they reviewed that of William Young, an ex-private of Sappers & Miners, who had been granted £7 10s in 1870 for the loss of his right arm during the siege of Sevastapol. They decided to award him an additional £13.

All this work meant that the Trustees were now meeting once a week and had to take on extra staff – a temporary assistant secretary, a lady 'type-writer' and an office boy to start with. Luckily, the Fund had moved offices in April 1899, its new premises being on the second floor of Brooke House, Walbrook. This boasted a lift, which was obviously much appreciated by disabled clients, a significant number of whom visited the office in person. By the end of December 1901, the office staff had risen to nine; the maximum number at any point in the

Patriotic Fund's history and three more rooms in Brooke House had to be rented.

In recognition of the part being played by Empire forces in South Africa, the Trustees made a donation of £1,000 to Canada in April 1900 and subsequently made similar donations to other dominions so that they could help their men in the same way. This triggered the establishment of Patriotic Funds by each dominion country. At this same meeting on 4 April, the Trustees made their first individual awards to the wounded from South Africa. These were not so much to help disabled men resettle into civilian life, but to tide them over until their pensions could be organised by the War Office. In this instance, the Fund made grants of £5 each to three soldiers and a marine. One was to a private soldier in the Duke of Cornwall's Light Infantry, who never actually reached South Africa. He caught a chill whilst waiting to embark at Southampton and was subsequently invalided out of the Army. At one meeting the following month, the Trustees made no less than 52 grants, totalling £225. In September, the number of South African War grants rose to 142 at a single meeting – a measure of how hard the Trustees and the Fund's office staff had to work. The Trustees also became concerned over the plight of wounded soldiers returning from South Africa who were awaiting arrears of pay. The War Office had laid down that they should apply to their commanding officers at home, but it would seem that their letters were going unanswered. The Trustees therefore made an agreement that any such cases coming to their notice would be communicated direct to the War Office.

Requests for help from other charities continued to come in to the Fund's office. Lady Hope asked for money to help establish a 'soldiers' hotel or club' in London, especially for those on sick leave. The Trustees declined to assist on the grounds that they were interested only in the sick and disabled from South Africa, while Lady Hope's project would have catered for all soldiers. They had more sympathy for a fund started by Lady Dudley for the assistance of officers and decided to grant her £1,000 to be used for those who were permanently disabled and on the understanding that the maximum award to each was to be £50. The Trustees also agreed to pay for each man discharged from the military hospital at Netley as unfit for further service to receive a greatcoat. Colonel Sir James Gildea, the founder of SSFA, also set up his Homes for Widows and Orphans of Officers, and the Fund supported five of the initial 12 ladies admitted to them.

By autumn 1900, the Boers had been thrown on the defensive. Kitchener and Roberts had been sent out to South Africa and during the spring and summer had invaded Orange Free State and Transvaal, raising the sieges of Kimberley, Ladysmith, and Mafeking. But, as the Boers reverted to guerrilla tactics, the war was not yet won and was to drag on for another 18 months. British forces were also involved in conflicts elsewhere. In China a secret organisation within the government had risen in revolt against foreign missionaries and Western interests in the country. The Boxers, as they were known, laid siege to the foreign legations in Peking. An international force, including British troops and sailors, was despatched to crush the uprising. Simultaneously, there was further unrest among the Ashanti tribe in West Africa.

Lloyd's Patriotic Fund felt that the public's attention should be drawn to the plight of those servicemen who suffered during these conflicts. After the Lord Mayor declined to initiate a subscription, the Fund launched its own, pointing out in its announcement that the naval brigade serving in China had already incurred 80 men killed and 240 wounded, of whom ten had already been invalided. The subscription was not a significant success, raising less than £500. The public focus remained on South Africa and, in any event, there had already been too many calls on people's pockets. Nonetheless, the Fund was able to provide some assistance to those who became casualties and their families, but it would be the last time that it attempted to raise its own public subscription.

With regard to grants for the disabled, among the early cases was a private of the Northamptonshire Regiment, who was suffering from a deformed big toe caused by long marches. He was given £5 to purchase a pair of surgical boots. Another private, this time from the Northumberland Fusiliers, had been discharged after suffering a gunshot wound to his arm and shell splinters in his back. The Fund gave him

British troops in action in South Africa. More than 75,000 were invalided home, sick or wounded.
Photograph: Courtesy of the Director, © NATIONAL ARMY MUSEUM, London.

£20 so that he could become a partner in his father's pianoforte business. The Trustees also gave £18 each to two privates of the Middlesex Regiment so that they could buy a phonograph and cylinders in order to enter the entertainment business. Others were each given a suit of clothes so that they could enter domestic service or tools to get them started in a trade.

A number of men were entered in the Corps of Commissionaires, but the Trustees soon discovered that some of them were resigning after a few days. The Corps was reimbursing them with the entry fee, which had been provided by the Fund, and the ex-soldier was promptly pocketing it. The Trustees therefore gave instructions that the fee was not to be refunded if the man's reasons for leaving were not sound and he himself was made to sign a certificate acknowledging this.

There were cases over which the Trustees had to wrestle with their consciences. One concerned a Coldstream Guards sergeant who had been discharged from the Army suffering from secondary syphilis. The Trustees' instinct was to turn down his application – they had already done this to a Grenadier Guards sergeant who had a similar complaint. But they learned that the ex-Coldstreamer had suffered from both dysentery and enteric in South Africa, had no pension, and was likely to die soon. They awarded him £5.

Besides the money from the Mansion House Fund, which, including interest, had risen to £125,000 by July, Lloyd's Patriotic Fund did receive other monies during the South African War. The first was 1,000 guineas from the will of Lieutenant Hugh Stewart McCorquodale who was killed in South Africa while serving with Thorneycroft's Mounted Infantry, one of the many irregular units formed. He had bequeathed this sum for charitable purposes and his brother felt that Lloyd's Patriotic Fund would be a more than appropriate recipient. McCorquodale's brother laid down that the

money be invested and the interest used to assist 'two men disabled by wounds, disease or accident in the present campaign in South Africa and discharged the service in consequence'. The first man to be made a grant from the McCorquodale fund was ex-Trooper Parker of Rimington's Scouts, another irregular unit, who had been partially paralysed after being wounded in the spine during the Modder River fighting. He was initially awarded £15.

Another bequest came from Miss Eliza Warrington of Malvern Wells, who left one-third of her personal estate to the Fund, again for disabled servicemen, but not just in connection with South Africa. The sum turned out to be nearly £9,500, but she had also left £100 for the erection of a window in the Parish Church of Hanley Castle in memory of her brother and herself. Unfortunately, the bill for the window exceeded the bequest and so the legatees were asked to make of the difference. The Trustees gladly agreed that the Fund should pay its share. Another more awkward situation then arose. A letter was received from the Blind College, Powycke in Worcestershire stating that Miss Warrington had been giving money for building work, which was as yet unfinished. The college authorities asserted that had she not died she would have provided more to ensure completion of the work and asked that the Fund donate £500. The Trustees turned down the request.

In January 1902, the Trustees submitted a report to the Lord Mayor on the South African Fund. They commented: 'The work involved extending over two years, and which still shows no sign of abatement – has been incessant and arduous, but of deep, if painful interest.' As for the officers and men which the Fund had helped, 'however grievous their condition, it has disclosed a spirit of cheerful fortitude which commands admiration and respect.' It went on to state that almost every man discharged disabled in Britain from the forces had been helped by the Fund. Indeed, of the total of 5,899

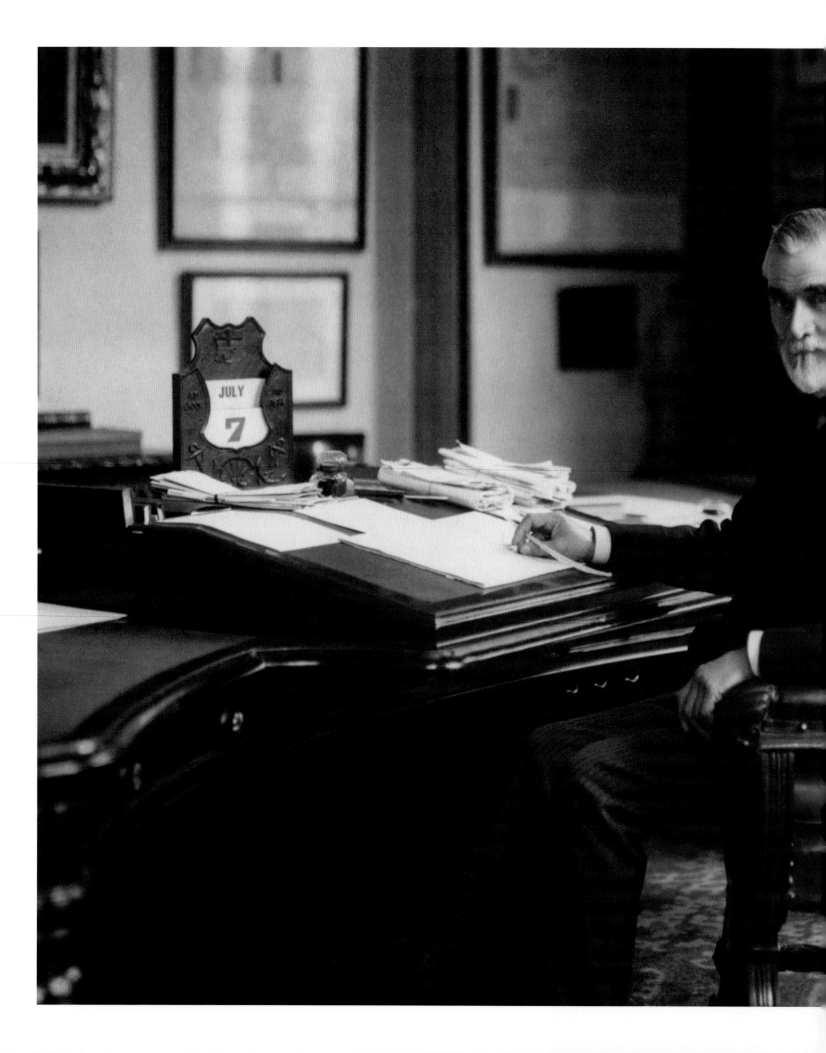

men officially declared discharged disabled as at 31 May 1902, the Fund had given assistance to 4,802. Weekly allowances made through 'responsible persons' had been given to those who were awaiting back pay and pension payments until such time as they received them or were in full employment. It was providing clothing for those discharged from hospital. The Fund was also helping to support workshops to teach the men trades. It was particularly interested in one in Dublin, since unemployment in the south of Ireland was high and Irish regiments had suffered heavy casualties in South Africa. Further assistance was being given to the Abercorn and Dudley Funds and to the Prince Christian Victor Memorial Fund. Prince Christian Victor himself was a grandson of Queen Victoria and a professional Army officer, who died of enteric in South Africa in 1900. The fund established in his memory was used to set up cottage homes for disabled soldiers. All in all, the Trustees could be proud of the work that they were doing and recognition of it was not long in coming.

Charles Wigram had given up the chairmanship of the Fund in April 1901 on the grounds of ill health, but the following year he was knighted for 'services in connection with the South African War'. This undoubtedly reflected the sterling efforts that Lloyd's Patriotic Fund had been making to relieve suffering. Sadly, Wigram himself passed away in 1903. The new chairman was Herbert de Rougemont, who had been a Trustee since 1889. Like the Sheddens before them, the de Rougemont family was to enjoy a close connection with the Fund, which lasts to this day.

In May 1902 the Boer War was finally brought to an end through the Treaty of Vereeniging. As a result of collections made at subsequent services of thanksgiving, the Fund received £1,000.

The war had highlighted the need for Service charities as never before and once more the example set by Lloyd's Patriotic Fund, the oldest of them, was being followed by others. But the Trustees, as ever, were never prepared to sit back on their laurels and the work of the Fund continued.

One particular concern was that while there was still plenty of money in the South African Fund, the interest on the General Fund, which supported the victims of other wars, was hard pressed to support new cases. Indeed, in April 1902, the Trustees had to impose a temporary freeze because of an overspend the previous financial year. The cost of presentations to the various schools the Fund supported was another problem area. True, the Royal Naval School at Eltham was dissolved in 1911, its buildings today being occupied by Goldsmiths' College, University of London, but the Fund was still supporting 114 pupils at five other institutions. To help maintain them, the Trustees decided towards the end of 1912 to publish a notice in The Times requesting donations. This helped to ease the strain and enabled the Fund to continue to meet its commitments. Nevertheless, as the new century wore on and political tensions increased in Europe, bringing threat of a major conflagration, the Trustees began to think how best they could utilise the Fund so that it would provide the same level of support as it had done during the South African War.

Chapter Seven

THE TWO WORLD WARS 1914–45

The tensions that had been gathering in Europe came to a head in July 1914 after the assassination of the Archduke Franz Ferdinand and his wife by a Serbian separatist in Sarajevo in the Austro-Hungarian province of Bosnia-Hercegovina. The members of the two great alliances in Europe at that time – the Central Alliance of Germany and Austria-Hungary, and the Triple Entente of Russia, France and Britain – mobilised. That of Austria-Hungary against Serbia was countered by Russia mobilising to protect fellow Slavs. This led Germany to do the same and France to mobilise in support of its Russian ally. Only Britain remained hesitant on the sidelines, but the German invasion of Belgium settled the issue. Citing an 1839 treaty guaranteeing Belgium's autonomy, the British Government delivered an ultimatum to Berlin. It was ignored and on 4 August Britain found herself at war.

Two days after Britain's declaration of war, the Prince of Wales announced the establishment of a National Relief Fund whose objective was the alleviation of both military and civilian distress resulting from the conflict. Within two months more than £3 million had been raised. The Lord Mayor of London had intended to raise a fund similar to that for the South African War, but cancelled his plans in the light of the National Relief Fund.

The Trustees of Lloyd's Patriotic Fund proposed that monies from this new fund be passed to them to administer, but this was declined by the management of the National Relief Fund on the grounds that they did not know at that stage what the demands on the fund would be. Lloyd's Patriotic Fund was therefore left somewhat in limbo, although its normal work continued. It also received some individual donations totalling some £630, which the Trustees termed the European War Relief Fund and began to use it to help men disabled in the war.

In April 1915, Lloyd's, which had set up its own war fund, handed over the administration of it to the Trustees of Lloyd's Patriotic Fund. The £115,000 raised was to be used for the benefit of Royal Navy and Royal Marine officers and it was agreed that four members of Lloyd's War Fund Committee would become additional Trustees of the Patriotic Fund. The new fund was initially called the 'Naval Officers War Fund' and its primary objective was assisting the education of the children of those killed in action. At the same time, the General Fund absorbed the small European War Relief Fund. It was then decided that the Naval Officers War Fund should be split, with £100,000 being dedicated to the Navy and the balance going to the Army. These became known respectively as X and Y Funds.

In November 1915, the Trustees drew up some guidelines as to whom they should be helping. Bearing in mind that there were numerous other charities, including the National Relief Fund, and reasonable pensions now being paid (as well as the

fact that Lloyd's Patriotic Fund possessed only limited funds), they decided that it was undesirable to give assistance, except in very special circumstances, to childless widows, dependent relations or disabled officers, unless the last-named had children. No help would be given if it would increase the family income to over 75 per cent of what it was on the officer's death. Also the maximum grant to a family would be limited to a quarter of the total government pension being drawn by it. Finally, grants to children would be limited to those under 13, since there were government education grants available to those above that age.

This was the last significant decision the Trustees took under the chairmanship of Herbert de Rougemont. He resigned that December because of his failing health and died the following October. De Rougemont, like his predecessors, devoted much time and trouble to the Fund. In 1903 he had written its centenary history and the

following year had become chairman of Lloyd's. Percy Janson, whose father was a Trustee for 30 years, succeeded him; he himself having been elected a Trustee on his father's death in 1910. Janson was also a cousin of Herbert de Rougemont.

The Trustees made their first grants from the X and Y Funds at a meeting held on 3 December 1915. Awards, ranging from £20 to £72, were made to the families of 42 naval and marine officers and one Army officer. Many were as a result of an incident off the Dutch coast on 22 September 1914, when the German submarine U9 sank three elderly British cruisers, *Aboukir*, *Cressy*, and *Hogue*. Sixty-two officers and 1,397 men perished in this disaster. They also made grants from the General Fund and others from the Transvaal or South African Fund, applicants for which were still coming forward.

The following September grants from the X Fund began to be made to the families of

The Loos Memorial and Dud Corner Cemetery, 5km northwest of Lens. Edwin Mackintosh's name is one of 25,000 commemorated who were killed in the area and have no known grave. *Photograph: © RICHARD HOWELLS of www.weforenglanddied.co.uk*

Percy Janson, Chairman of Lloyd's Patriotic Fund 1915-1927. The sub-fund that bears his name still operates. *Photograph: © MRS DAWN LAMBERT*

the victims of Jutland, the one major fleet action of the war, when the Grand Fleet clashed with the German High Seas Fleet on 31 May 1916. In terms of losses, the Royal Navy came off worst, losing, among other vessels, three of its prized battle cruisers, but strategically it was a British victory in that it deterred the German fleet from leaving port for the remainder of the war.

October 1916 saw a new fund created as part of Lloyd's Patriotic Fund. Lieutenant Edwin Hampson Mackintosh, the son of a ship owner, was a Kitchener volunteer who joined the 8th Black Watch shortly after the outbreak of war. He was killed on 25 September, the first day of the Battle of Loos. In his will, he left his sister Lillian £1,000 to be used for charitable purposes in connection with the Army and the same amount for the Royal Navy. In a letter to the Trustees dated 27 October, Mrs Broad stated that she had decided to pass the latter to Lloyd's Patriotic Fund. 'I do not wish to define too closely the use to which the interest of this investment shall be put, but would desire to leave its distribution to the discretion of the Trustees of Lloyd's Patriotic Fund, provided only that it shall be used for the benefit of Officers of the Royal Navy and their dependent sufferers by the present war to have first consideration.' Edwin Mackintosh himself has no known grave, but his name is commemorated on the Loos Memorial.

At the same meeting at which the new fund was discussed, the Trustees considered a request from the Lloyd's Mutual Aid Society, which looked after the welfare of the Lloyd's community, that it should give some help to its Members and their dependants who had been killed or wounded. The Trustees, concerned that their funds were limited, did not take an immediate decision, but did eventually decide to dedicate the Y Fund to the Lloyd's community.

Lloyd's as a whole did much more for the war effort than merely raise its War Fund. In March 1916 it presented ambulances to the French, a gift much appreciated at the time since the French Army was locked in the desperate defence of the historic fortress town of Verdun in the face of a major German offensive. More than £100,000 was given to Red Cross societies and £46,000 to the Young Men's Christian Association (YMCA) for the erection of canteens and recreation rooms for the forces.

In April 1915 Lloyd's established a fund to reward the crews of merchant vessels who had, through their own efforts, successfully evaded attacks by U-boats. A total of just over £17,700 was collected during the war and sums of up to £250 awarded to the crews. Lloyd's also continued to award its Medal for Saving Life. Finally, no less than 215 Members of the Lloyd's community laid down their lives for their country during 1914–18.

When the Armistice, bringing the fighting finally to an end, was signed on 11 November 1918, it was revealed that Lloyd's Patriotic Fund had, since its inception in 1803, made grants in excess of one million pounds. The demands on it during the war had, however, been heavy and economies needed to be made. In February 1919, it was decided to limit the awards to officers' widows and children: £26 to widows, £26 for the first child, and £13 to the second. Each case would be reviewed annually.

A year later, the Trustees decided that the X Fund was in such a poor state that it was unable to help naval officers disabled during 1914-18 and that they would have to impose a temporary freeze on new applications for help from the General Fund. True, some money did come in. The Baltic and Lloyd's Ambulance Unit donated £1,000 when it wound up its accounts in 1919 and a similar sum was given by King George's Fund for Sailors, which had been founded in 1917. Two Members of Lloyd's even gave £15 which they had earned driving their cars on government business during the war.

However, the most significant donation came from the chairman himself. Percy Janson presented £10,000 in 5-per-cent war loans and it was agreed that the interest from it should be used primarily for the education and maintenance of the children of officers of all three Services. In 1924 he also made an agreement with the Members of Lloyd's that they should make an annual donation to the Patriotic Fund. That same year the Fund also received £2,000 from the unappropriated portion of the prize money payable by the Admiralty on captured enemy vessels during 1914-18. Janson himself died in February 1927, while still in office, and was succeeded as chairman by Charles de Rougemont, a cousin of Herbert.

The Trustees' meeting at which Charles de Rougemont was elected chairman provides a useful snapshot of the work of Lloyd's Patriotic Fund at that time.

❖ Fifty-three annuities from War Fund X to naval officers' widows were renewed for a further year and two discontinued, since there had been an improvement in the finances of the ladies concerned.

❖ Under War Fund Y there were four renewals of annuities to the widows of an Army NCO, a private, a former air mechanic in the Royal Flying Corps, and an ex-Sapper in the Royal Engineers.

❖ There were a further 73 renewals under the General Fund and four new cases were considered. These resulted in awards of £26 each to the daughters of a deceased lieutenant colonel in the Royal Marine Light Infantry, a com-

People, many of them in mourning, pass Sir Edward Lutyens' newly unveiled Cenotaph, Whitehall on Armistice Day 1920. *Photograph: © IMPERIAL WAR MUSEUM Q31494*

mander RN, and an Indian Army captain, and a similar sum to the widow of a paymaster RN, and one of £13 to a petty officer's widow.

❖ Twenty-six pounds each were granted from the Janson Fund to the widow of a captain in the Bechuanaland Police, the widowed daughter of a deceased lieutenant colonel in the 28th Regiment, and the daughter of a late rear admiral.

❖ Four former NCOs and privates received £13 each from the Warrington Fund, and a major late of the 59th Regiment, £26.

❖ The South African Fund also paid out grants ranging from £4 2s 6d to £52 to eight former NCOs and junior ranks of the Army. The Trustees then went on to decide on nine nominations for the Royal Hospital School.

❖ Finally, they reviewed the situation of the various funds as at the end of 1926.

It was as follows:

Fund	Capital	Grants in 1926
General	£85,670	£4072 12s 5d
McCorquodale	£1097 3s 1d	£25 5s 0d
Warrington	£11,437	£26 5s 0d
Mackintosh	£975 4s 3d	£54
Janson	£10,124 6s 2d	£489
South African	£21,674 14 0d	£794 8s 6d
War Fund X	£56,111 1s 10d	£7,930
War Fund Y	£19,139 13s 1d	£740 10s 0d

All in all, the meeting covered much ground, but it was typical of the time, with meetings being held quarterly.

In September 1927 the then Secretary, Lt Col A N St Quintin, resigned after being in the post since March 1915. He had laboured tirelessly to maintain the Fund's administration on an even keel and had been made an Officer of the Order of the British Empire for his services. He had also, at his own expense, written and published a limited edition history of Lloyd's Patriotic Fund, donating all proceeds from its sales to the Fund. On his retirement, he was given the singular honour of being appointed a Trustee.

At that time, the Fund's offices were also about to move from Brooke House. Lloyd's itself had returned to the Royal Exchange, which had been rebuilt after the great fire of 1838, in 1844. In 1923, the Committee of Lloyd's acquired a prime site in the City of London, more than three quarters of acre of ground on which the old East India House, headquarters of the Honourable East India Company, had stood. It had good frontages on both Leadenhall Street and Lime Street and was the ideal place for a purpose-built home for Lloyd's.

HM King George V laid the foundation stone in May 1925 and just under three years later, Lloyd's New Building opened and there was room available for Lloyd's Patriotic Fund to have two rooms as offices for the Secretary and his two assistants at a very reasonable rent. It was also agreed that the Trustees could hold their meetings in one of the committee rooms at no extra charge. Thus, after well over 100 years of geographical separation, the Fund was back under the roof of the institution that had spawned it.

By 1928 the Fund was in a very much better state than it had been eight years earlier, and the Trustees decided to rescind the rule that the widows of those who had died of disease aggravated or induced by war should be ineligible for grants. At much the same time, the Trustees noted that what they were now calling the Great War Fund (Military), formerly War Fund Y, had not all been expended on Lloyd's community cases and so they decided to extend it to cover other military cases. They also received an additional £1,000 from the Royal Navy's Prize Fund, which was allocated to the Mackintosh Fund.

Also in 1929, £100 was received from the proceeds of that year's Royal Tournament. A sum from this source would be paid annually into Lloyd's Patriotic Fund until after the start of the Second World War. Other military tattoos, notably those at Aldershot and Tidworth, also made contributions. Among the other gifts in 1929 was an anonymous one, consisting of £108 in bank notes. The Trustees thanked the donor, whoever he or she might have been, by placing notices in *The Times* and *Lloyd's List*. The same happened in June 1940, although the amount involved was somewhat smaller, being just £15.

One unusual gift, made in 1930, was a cottage near Market Harborough, which the donor specified should be for the use of a Patriotic Fund beneficiary of the officer class or 'superior rank and file case'. The Trustees had great difficulty in finding someone to live in it, especially since the only person who showed any interest declined the offer after viewing the cottage. They were therefore forced to accept failure and return it to the owner.

The following year, Charles de Rougemont was paid a touching compliment. The United Service Club made him an honorary member 'in grateful acknowledgement of the long continued and generous sympathy extended by Lloyd's and its Patriotic Fund to Officers and Men of the Fighting Services and their Dependents who have suffered in the many wars in which this country has been engaged during the last 128 years'. Lloyd's Patriotic Fund had a valuable collection of Nelson's papers, as well as other artefacts from the era, including Patriotic Fund swords and vases. Lloyd's also had a collection of plate and other items and it was decided that a permanent display should be mounted. Hence, on Trafalgar Day 1931 the Nelson Room was opened at Lloyd's as a memorial to the close relationship that had existed between Horatio Nelson and the Fund.

Another link with that bygone era came in 1928 when the Fund made a special grant to an 88-year-old lady, whose grandfather had fought as a midshipman on board HMS *Temeraire* at Trafalgar. On the other hand, an application made in 1933 by an Underwriter for help for the great great granddaughter of Admiral Rodney, victor over the French at the Battle of the Saints in 1782 during the latter stages of the American War of Independence, was rejected. The Trustees turned it down on the grounds that only immediate dependants of former servicemen were eligible for benefits and in this case the woman's father was a civil servant.

At the same meeting, the Trustees also had to deal with a complaint made to the Charity Commission. It concerned a man who had been discharged as unfit from the Army in 1901 and had recently failed in his application for help from the South African Fund. He was turned down because he was actually asking for compensation for being unemployed rather than for the disability that he had suffered for 30 years. The Trustees explained this to the Charity Commission and nothing more was heard.

The Fund's interest in the schools with which it had close connections was maintained. A meeting in June 1932 noted that it had its full entitlement of 30 nominations at the Royal United Service Orphan Home for Girls at Devonport, to which the Trustees also granted £100 towards the cost of acquiring a holiday home for the girls. Nominations were also still being made to the Royal Soldiers' Daughters Home at Hampstead, the Royal School Bath, the Royal Naval School at Twickenham, and the Royal Hospital School.

The Royal Hospital School moved from London in 1933. This was thanks to the generosity of Gifford Sherman Reade, who in 1921 presented land at Holbrook south of Ipswich to the Admiralty in gratitude for the protection given by the Royal Navy to his tea ships during the Great War. On his death in 1929, the Admiralty used the residue of his estate to build a school on the land and the Royal Hospital School moved. Its former premises in Greenwich were shortly taken over by the newly established National Maritime Museum, which occupies them to this day.

The facilities at the new school were certainly much better than those at Greenwich. All the equipment, too, was entirely new and the boys now wore naval uniform only on special occasions. There were, however, some drawbacks. All boys now had to wear shorts, which proved to be insufficient protection from the biting East Coast wind in winter. Discipline, too, was placed too much i n the hands of the boys. Consequently, there was initially some discontent, but matters soon settled down.

In 1930 the Fund had an additional call on its services. The Trustees were asked if they would act as almoners to St George's Home School for Officers' Children, which was closing down at the end of the summer term. The Fund received £2,000 to help the parents with the fees for the new schools, which they had selected for their offspring. The St George's Fund, as it was called, continued in existence until the end of 1968, by which time it was exhausted, and the remaining beneficiaries became the responsibility of the Janson Fund.

Because of the multiplicity of funds under the umbrella of Lloyd's Patriotic Fund, the Trustees decided in October 1932 to rationalise the purposes of the General Fund. They resolved that in future it would concentrate primarily on the families of those killed or wounded in conflicts prior to the Great War. The

second priority was the families of veterans of these wars who retired through ill health caused by their service, and the third for others who had served in any of these wars, but who had retired voluntarily or at the end of their term of service or through ill health not connected with their service. The final and lowest category was those without war service, but had been forced to retire because of ill health. The Members and Subscribers of Lloyd's were continuing to help keep the General Fund topped up with annual donations averaging some £1,600 under the arrangement made by Percy Janson.

But, as the 1930s drew on, Europe once more faced an increasing threat of war. The stridency of the Nazi regime in Germany and its determination to tear up the Treaty of Versailles and restore not just Germany's pre-1914 frontiers but create a Germanic empire in Europe made other nations fearful. In 1935 Britain slowly began to rearm. At the same time, efforts to appease Hitler in the hope that he might end his aggressive territorial expansion policy eventually failed. By the end of 1938, war seemed inevitable. Hitler had by now turned on Poland, determined to eradicate the Polish Corridor that, under Versailles, had isolated East Prussia from the remainder of Germany. Britain and France allied themselves with the Poles, who refused to give in to German threats.

In the midst of this, Charles de Rougemont died, like his predecessor, in harness. The mantle of the chairmanship of Lloyd's Patriotic Fund was placed on the shoulders of Sir Percy Mackinnon, one of the giants of Lloyd's at the time. He had been Lloyd's chairman no less than five times during 1925–33 and had been the driving force behind Lloyd's New Building. The Fund would therefore be in good hands as it faced a second major war almost within a generation.

The Royal School, Twickenham (top) and the girls of Drake House, 1923 (bottom). Lloyd's Patriotic Fund helped with the school fees of those whose fathers had been killed or disabled while serving in the Royal Navy and Royal Marines.
Photograph: © ROYAL SCHOOL, Haslemere

When Britain did declare war on Germany on 3 September 1939, the mood of the country was very different to that of August 1914. Then there had been a wave of popular enthusiasm; now there was just grim acceptance. There was no national fund initiated, as in 1914. It was partly the mood of the country, but also because Service charities were now better established and government pensions reasonable. In addition, while Poland was fighting for its life, little was happening in the West. The Phoney War, as an American journalist termed it, seemed to be somewhat of a letdown.

In this atmosphere, the Trustees understandably had no wish to raise any subscription as they had done in the past and just carried on with the normal work of the Fund. That October, the Central Bureau of Naval Officers' Charities did ask the Fund to assist in cases of distress caused by deaths in the war. The Trustees, fully conscious that Poland had now been crushed, but that inactivity continued in the West, were not prepared to commit themselves, since no one knew what the level of casualties might be in the future. They did, however, agree to consider individual cases 'as far as the limited funds at present available will permit'.

In March 1940 the situation with regard to formulating new policy for the Fund became clearer when it received £1,730 for the education of the children of naval officers killed in action. Sir Percy Mackinnon proposed that £9,000 from the Naval War Fund and £11,000 from the Military War Fund be added to this sum to create Lloyd's Naval Scholarships. At the Trustees' next meeting in June it was decided to set up the Naval War Fund 1940 to assist the widows of naval officers and that £3,000 should be transferred from the Naval and Military War Funds. Twenty Naval Scholarships of £50 and twenty of £20 per annum for five years would be established.

However, the Charity Commission then stepped in, ruling that it was unlawful to transfer money from the Military War Fund to the Naval War Fund 1940. This caused a certain amount of confusion, especially since nine awards to widows had already been made from it. It would seem that, as a result of this, the Trustees decided to dissolve the Naval War Fund 1940 and merely use the existing Naval and Military War Funds.

September 1940 witnessed the beginning of the Blitz, the German bombing campaign against London and other cities, which would continue until the following May. An early casualty was the Secretary to the Fund, Brigadier General William Usher Smith CB CBE DSO, who was killed with his wife on 16 September. He had won his DSO in the South African War and had ended the Great War as Director of Ordnance Services in Salonika. He had served the Fund faithfully since taking over from Colonel St Quintin in 1927. A replacement was appointed on probation, but he proved to be unsuitable. Luckily, the Fund was able to obtain the services of S W Burghes, who had just retired as Principal Clerk to the Corporation of Lloyd's, and he served as Secretary for the remainder of the war.

In 1941 there was a new development. Lloyd's had raised nearly £85,000 for the alleviation of distress among airmen and their dependants. The Trustees of the Patriotic Fund proposed that they take over a portion of this and use it to deal with RAF Coastal Command and Fleet Air Arm cases, together with all RAF Members of the Lloyd's community. Lloyd's passed over the complete subscription and the Fund then came to an agreement with the RAF Benevolent Fund that it would pass over relevant cases for the Trustees to deal with. The Patriotic Fund began to make grants from the Corporation of Lloyd's Air Force Fund in December 1941. A few months

on, it became clear that the RAF Benevolent Fund's Coastal Command cases were being submitted to the Trustees with claims for considerably more money than they were prepared to pay out. They therefore decided to pass £50,000 across to the RAF Benevolent Fund for Coastal Command cases on the proviso that Lloyd's Patriotic Fund would have a seat on the Benevolent Fund's General Council and one on its Grants Committee.

This left the Trustees with just the Fleet Air Arm cases and those concerning Lloyd's staff serving in the RAF. This system appears to have worked well and the Air Force Fund continued to operate until 1961, when it was finally exhausted. The remaining cases from it were transferred to the Naval War Fund.

The Trustees continued making their nominations to the various schools, but in the case of the Royal Hospital School they experienced much difficulty in filling their quota of 60 pupils at the school.

It was still controlled by the Director of Greenwich Hospital at the Admiralty and his view was that parents preferred to keep their sons at home because of Holbrooke's position on the coast, which put it very much in the front line; not that it ever came under attack.

During the Second World War there were two unique donations to Lloyd's Patriotic Fund. In 1942 it received a bequest from a James Edwards, who had died two years earlier. He had served as a private in the East Surrey Regiment and been badly wounded. The Fund gave him some help and Edwards reflected his gratitude in his will. Apart from two small legacies, his estate was to be shared between his Regimental Association and the Lloyd's Patriotic Fund, whose share was £330. The other donation was in the summer of 1945. The New York firm of Duncan & Mount made a gift of $5,000 to the Committee of Lloyd's 'to be used for such British Charitable purposes as in the sole judgement of the Committee will best serve present or future needs. This contribution is made as small tribute to magnificent part played by Great Britain during European War, now happily terminated, and as recognition of work done, and being done, in Asiatic War.' The Committee divided the money between King George's Fund for Sailors and Lloyd's Patriotic Fund.

Sir Percy MacKinnon remained on the Committee of the Lloyd's Patriotic Fund and it was at his instigation that Lloyd's introduced a new medal at the end of 1940. This was Lloyd's War Medal for Bravery at Sea, which was instituted with the approval of both the Admiralty and the Ministry of Shipping and recognised the courage of merchant seamen in the face of hostile action. The obverse had an 'heroic figure', which symbolised 'courage and endurance', while the trident on the reverse represented sea power. The trident was surrounded by laurels and acorns, suggesting 'those qualities of sturdiness and endurance which are as present in our seamen who serve in ships of steel as ever they were in their predecessors who manned the "Wooden Walls of Old England".

The first awards, to 54 men from 31 ships, were announced in Lloyd's List & Shipping Gazette on 31 March 1941, and during the course of the war a total of 530 awards were made, including five to women, as well as allied seamen from Denmark, Norway, Belgium and the Netherlands. Apart from the money it raised for charitable purposes and this new medal, the Lloyd's community, as it had done during 1914-18, also took an active part in the war, with many serving in the Armed forces. There are 218 of them recorded in Lloyd's Book of Remembrance as having fallen.

Lloyd's Medal for Bravery at Sea in gold. Together with its silver and bronze versions, it was Lloyd's way of demonstrating its admiration for the courage and devotion of the crews of the Merchant Navy in time of war. *Photograph: © LLOYD'S*

Chapter Eight

PAST, PRESENT AND FUTURE
1945 onwards

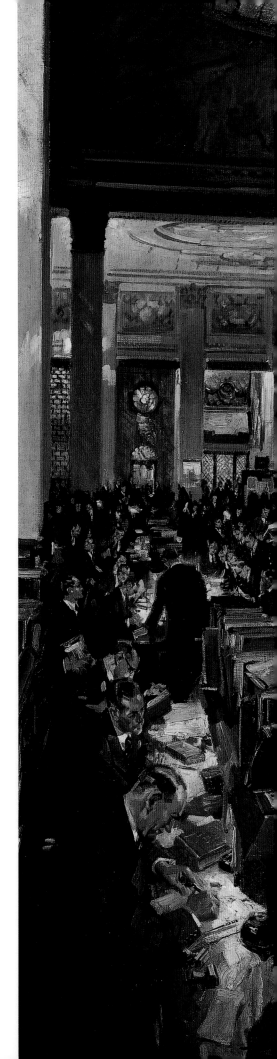

The cost of living had risen significantly during the war years and this was reflected in school fees. In the autumn of 1947 the Trustees of Lloyd's Patriotic Fund received a request from the Royal Naval School, which had moved from Twickenham to Haslemere during the war, requesting that it increase the £36 per annum paid for each of the Fund's two nominations. The Fund raised the sum to £56. The following year there was a similar request from the Royal School Bath. In this instance the Trustees asked to see the school's accounts for 1947 before coming to a decision. Having inspected these, they agreed to an additional £30 per annum for each of the five nominations.

The Trustees were also continuing to make nominations of the sons of former merchant seamen to the Royal Hospital School, Holbrook. The Admiralty had, however, ceased to expect boys leaving the school to enter the Royal Navy. Nominations for the other institutions gradually fell by the wayside as these schools were wound up. For instance, the last recorded nominations for the Royal United Service Home for Girls, which had moved from Devonport to Newquay, were made in 1955.

The main work of the Fund, that of looking after the dependants of deceased servicemen and former servicemen themselves, continued unabated. Indeed, at the beginning of 1955 the Trustees noted that their work had trebled since 1939. January of that year saw Sir Percy Mackinnon step down after nearly 16 years as chairman.

Ernest de Rougemont, son of Charles, succeeded him. He had been a Trustee since 1934 and was appointed the Fund's representative on the RAF Benevolent Fund's Grants Committee in 1946, subsequently serving on its General Council. His services to charity would shortly be recognised when he was made a CBE in the 1959 New Year's Honours. The Secretary throughout this time was Mrs L R Spicer (née Wiggett), whose service to the Fund had begun in 1919, when she joined the office staff. She took over as Secretary in 1947 and did not retire until 1963.

Apart from the odd bequest, the Fund was reliant on the annual donation made to it by Lloyd's Charities Trust. This enabled it to increase grants in line with the cost of living. Thus, in 1956 it was able to increase the annuities made to officers' widows and dependants from £40 to £46 per annum and those of the remainder from £20 to £26. A further boost to finances came in 1956 with a donation of £10,000 from King George's Fund for Sailors. This was placed in the Naval War Fund. At the end of 1965 the Trustees noted that the last beneficiary from the South African Fund had died. The fund continued to be used to cover other cases and was not finally closed until 1976, when the 23 cases being supported by it were transferred to the General Fund.

In the meantime, in 1966 the Trustees successfully applied to the Charity Commissioners for a Certificate of Incorporation by which the capital stock of the Fund was returned to Lloyd's.

The number of cases dealt with in 1969 was 321 renewals of annual grants and 51 special 'one off' grants. As people passed on, so the number of renewals declined, as did new applications, and by 1979 the Trustees were holding just two meetings per year.

By this time, David Beck had taken over as chairman, although Ernest de Rougemont remained a Trustee until 1988. The new chairman's father had served as a Trustee during the Great War years and was the first recipient of Lloyd's Medal for Services to Lloyd's in gold. This award had been instituted in 1913 to recognise outstanding contributions to the Corporation and consists of three classes – gold, silver and bronze. David Beck himself became an Underwriter in 1937. A keen Territorial soldier, he had been commissioned into the Royal Artillery from the Honourable Artillery Company on the day before Britain declared war in 1939 and served throughout the war years. In 1981 he sold his father's gold medal and donated the proceeds to the Patriotic Fund.

Another change at this time was that the administrative work for the Fund was placed under the jurisdiction of the Corporation of Lloyd's. This came about with the appointment of Jim Gawler as Secretary in July 1980. He was already in Lloyd's employ and undertook his new duties in conjunction with his existing responsibilities. This meant a not insignificant saving on the Fund's overheads.

On 26 October 1981, Kenneth Howorth, a Scotland Yard bomb disposal expert and holder of the George Medal, was killed while trying to defuse an IRA bomb that had been placed by the Provisional IRA in a restaurant in London's Oxford Street. Lloyd's Patriotic Fund made a donation of £250 to the fund set up in his memory. The following year the community of Lloyd's raised a subscription 'as a mark of the esteem in which all our Armed forces, as exemplified by those engaged in the South Atlantic, are held by the Lloyd's community'. It was stressed that this was entirely separate to the South Atlantic Fund, which had been raised on a national basis, and the £21,710 collected was passed to Lloyd's Patriotic Fund for general use rather than specifically for Falklands War veterans and their dependants.

At the same time, the Fund established close links with the British Limbless Ex-Servicemen's Association (BLESMA), which had been founded in 1932 to look after casualties of the Great War. In 1982 the Trustees arranged the donation of 100 Christmas presents, each to the value of £100, to be given to those being cared for by the charity.

Indeed, by the early 1980s, the Trustees were working evermore closely with other charities. Most new cases were now coming via SSAFA, the Forces Help Society, and the Officers' Association, as well as from the Department of Health and Social Security. After a relative slump in the numbers of beneficiaries during the 1970s, the next decade saw a significant rise. In 1983 the Fund expended just under £31,400 in aid, but ten years later this sum had risen to more than £121,000. Much of the reason for this was that the veterans of the Second World War and their widows were now reaching old age and their needs were consequently more than they had been.

This phenomenon caused the Trustees to take another look at the structure of the Fund. They noted that 98 per cent of the grants were being made from the General Fund, but this had only 40 per cent of the Patriotic Fund's investments. In contrast, the Naval War Fund, which was being used mainly for the education of deceased Naval and Royal Marine officers' daughters at Haslemere, possessed 52 per cent of the investments. Thus, at the end of 1992 the Trustees decided to merge the two so as to provide more flexibility. However, the other sub-funds – McCorquodale, Mackintosh and Janson – could not legally be absorbed by the General Fund and had to retain their separate identities.

By this time, of course, the Corporation of Lloyd's had moved into its current premises. Growing business had necessitated the opening of a second building on Lime Street in 1958. By the late 1970s, however, the increasing number of syndicates and the need for a working environment more akin to the late 20th century led the Corporation to commission the architect Richard Rogers to design an entirely new building. It was opened by Her Majesty The Queen and His Royal Highness The Duke of Edinburgh in 1986.

The Underwriting Room is three times the size of its predecessor, but is still dominated by the Lutine Bell. This came from the French frigate *La Lutine*, which had been captured in 1793 only to sink off the Dutch coast six years later. She was carrying gold and silver bullion and the loss was borne by Lloyd's Underwriters. In 1858 her bell was recovered and later installed in the Underwriting Room. Up until 1981 it was rung once to announce overdue ships and twice when the ship was reported safe, but is now only sounded on special occasions; one of the most notable in recent years was to mark the New York Twin Towers disaster of 11 September 2001.

After 1993 the number of the Patriotic Fund's annuitants began to decline. There were a total of 424 in 1994, each person being granted between £100 and £520 per annum according to the degree of hardship being suffered. Each was renewed annually and, in some cases, an improvement in the beneficiary's financial circumstances led to the annuity being reduced or cancelled. The General Fund was paying the vast

majority of the grants and it was noticeable that most were going to former soldiers and their widows or other dependants. Annuities were being paid from the Janson Fund in the form of educational bursaries, as was one from the McCorquodale Fund, while the Mackintosh Fund remained dedicated to providing bursaries for the daughters of Naval officers and Royal Marines. The Patriotic Fund also made a considerable number of 'one off' grants.

At the Trustees' meeting held on 10 May 1994, no less than 169 of these were approved. The sums in question ranged from £50 to £100 and covered a wide range of needs. Some grants were towards the purchase of electric chairs and stair lifts. Others were used to help clear debts, carry out house repairs, and towards funeral expenses. Winter clothing and domestic appliances also featured. In one case, a grant of £75 was made to a man to cover the travel costs of his wife visiting him in hospital. The general principle adopted was that other Service charities would also contribute in each case, which they invariably did and continue to do. Apart from its investment income, the

Patriotic Fund continues to receive a number of bequests and donations. In November 1996, the late Guy Janson MBE, son of Percy, left the sum of £25,000 to the Fund in recognition of his family's close connection with it. The following year, the estate of Alfred Francis Deards passed over a legacy of £25,854. As for investments, in 1995 Kleinwort Benson took over the management of these, although this company would soon be taken over by Dresdener RCM Global Investors, which continues to look after them. The management aims to achieve maximum income in order to support the Fund's committed expenditure while preserving the capital in real terms.

In 1996 the Trustees were able to pass two additional bursaries, each of £1,250 per annum, to the Naval Scholarship Fund. At the same time they were able to offer an extra £1,250 bursary to the Royal School Bath. In 1997 the Gurkha Welfare Trust made a national appeal for additional money. Lloyd's Patriotic Fund donated £2,500, with an undertaking that, subject to an annual review, a similar sum would be handed over every year. This money is used to provide pensions for 21 Gurkha veterans

of the Second World War, whose period of service was insufficient to qualify them for an Army pension.

In 1998 the Trustees decided on a significant change of policy. A year earlier, the forces Help Society and Lord Roberts' Workshops, which had been established by Countess Meath in 1899 to help disabled servicemen from South Africa find employment, were merged with SSAFA to form SSAFA forces Help. The Trustees concluded that it would improve the efficiency of processing applications for grants if the administration was passed over to SSAFA. They initially agreed to hand over £30,000 in two tranches each year so that they could pay beneficiaries direct, but this was raised to £40,000 before the end of 1998. The main stipulation was that each 'one off' grant should not exceed £500. This system is still operating, with the Trustees and SSAFA jointly reviewing cases every six months.

At the same time, the Trustees decided not to grant any new annuities and to allow the existing ones to fade away naturally. By the end of 2002, the number of annuitants had fallen to less than 80, but the Trustees continue to pay close attention to them; in one instance making a grant of £30 for flowers on the occasion of one of them attaining the age of 100. With regard to education, the Trustees noted that in year 2000 no one was applying for bursaries to what was now called the Royal High School, Bath after an amalgamation between the Royal School and High School, Bath. The reason was that the parents of girls who might have been eligible were serving members of the Armed forces rather than former ones. The Trustees therefore decided that in future they would throw the net wider and not merely restrict bursaries to the Royal High School, Bath, the Royal Naval School and the Royal Hospital School.

The year 2003 marks the bicentennial year of Lloyd's Patriotic Fund. Apart from the publication of a new history of the Fund, the Trustees have decided on a new initiative. This is to restore the link forged with the Royal Air Force in the Second World War through Lloyd's Air Force Fund. This will once more make the Fund open to all three Armed Services.

Looking back over the past 200 years, Lloyd's Patriotic Fund can rightfully claim to be a major pioneer in the field of Service charities. The example that the Members of Lloyd's set when they established the Fund in 1803 served to inspire both Britain's Armed forces and the nation as a whole. In terms of history, the early years of the Fund are the most glamorous, with the Patriotic Fund quickly becoming a household name. From Waterloo onwards, others stepped in to share the burden of providing help for servicemen and their dependants and Lloyd's was content to play a smaller role. But the expertise that it has developed has proved invaluable to other charities.

Lloyd's Patriotic Fund, too, has for many years made it its business to ensure that former sailors, soldiers and airmen or their dependants are not forgotten when they fall on hard times. The scope of the Fund's operations may now be small compared with those of other Service charities, but they are no less valued.

As for the future, the veterans of the Second World War may now be dwindling, but Lloyd's Patriotic Fund remains busy providing help for those of the numerous conflicts in which Britain's Armed forces have been engaged since 1945. In the uncertain world of the 21st century, the demands on the Fund are certain to continue and the Royal Navy, Army and Royal Air Force will continue to be grateful for the long tradition of generous support which Lloyd's Patriotic Fund and the Lloyd's community as a whole have provided. Indeed, the willingness of the Lloyd's community to give charitable help is a characteristic of which it has long been proud.

Below: The annual remembrance ceremony for the members of the Lloyd's Community who gave their lives in the two world wars. Lloyd's Book of Remembrance contains 433 names. *Photograph: © NEWSCAST TBC*

Right: Royal Marines on the long march to Port Stanley, capital of the Falkland Islands, June 1982. The casualties of the Falklands War were specifically assisted by the nationally raised South Atlantic Fund rather than by Lloyd's Patriotic Fund. Lloyd's did, however, raise its own subscription which it passed to the Patriotic Fund. *Photograph: © Imperial War Museum FKD2028*

Lieutenant Charles Adams HMS Renomee
Cutting out the Spanish schooner Giganta at Veija, 4 May 1806 – £50 Sword

Brigadier General Sir Samuel Auchmuty
Capture of Monte Video, 3 February 1807 – £200 Vase

Captain Francis William Austen HMS Canopus
Action off San Domingo, 6 February 1806 – £100 Vase

Lieutenant Ayscough HMS Centaur
Destruction of a battery on Martinique, 26 November 1803 – £50 Sword

Major General Sir David Baird
Capture of the Cape of Good Hope, 10 January 1806 – £300 Vase

Captain Thomas Baker HMS Phoenix
Capture of the French frigate La Didon, 10 August 1805 – £100 Sword
Action off Ferrol, 4 November 1805 – £100 Vase

Captain Henry William Bayntun HMS Leviathan
Trafalgar, 21 October 1805 – £100 Sword

Lieutenant George Beattie Royal Marines HMS Blenheim
Capture of Fort Dunkirk, Martinique, 17 November 1803 – £50 Sword

Major General William Carr Beresford
Capture of Buenos Ayres, 2 July 1806 – £200 Vase

Captain Sir Edward Berry HMS Agamemnon
Trafalgar, 21 October 1805 – £100 Vase
Action off San Domingo, 6 February 1806 – £100 Vase

Lieutenant Bettesworth HMS Centaur
Capture of the French corvette Curieux, Martinique, 4 February 1804 – £50 Sword

Captain Austin Bissell HMS Racoon
Capture of French vessels off Cuba, 14 October 1803 – £100 Sword

Captain The Hon Henry Blackwood HMS Euryalus
Trafalgar, 21 October 1805 – £100 Sword

Lieutenant Bluett HM Sloop Scorpion
Capture of the Dutch vessel Atalante, 31 March 1804 – £50 Sword

Captain William Bolton HMS Fisgard
Capture of Curacao, 1 January 1807 – £100 Sword

Lieutenant Bowen HMS Loire
Cutting out French brig Venteux, Isle de Bas, 27 June 1803 – £50 Sword

Midshipman William Pitt Bowler HM Sloop Swift
Capture of Spanish schooner La Caridad Perfecta, Truxillo, 13 August 1805 – £30 Sword

Lieutenant Boxer HMS Antelope
Capture of a Dutch Schrik, 23 March 1804 – £50 Sword

Captain Brenton HMS Spartan
Gallant action against an enemy squadron, Mediterranean, 3 July 1810 – £100 Sword (*This award was made after the Patriotic Fund Committee had ceased making honorary awards, but because it passed through the books of the Fund's swordmaker and was paid for direct by the Fund, it is included in the main list*)

Captain Charles Brisbane HMS Arethusa
Attack on Moro Castle, Cuba, 23 August 1806 – £100 Sword* Capture of Curacao, 1 January 1807 – £200 Vase

Captain Robert Hunter Brown HEIC Ship Dorsetshire
Action of East India Company convoy against French naval squadron, Malacca Straits, 15 February 1804 – £50 Sword

Captain Charles Bullen HMS Britannia
Trafalgar, 21 October 1805 – £100 Sword

Lieutenant Canning HMS Desiree
Cutting out of five schooners and a sloop, Manchinelle, 18 August 1803 – £50 Sword

Captain The Hon Thomas Bladen Capel HMS Phoebe
Trafalgar, 21 October 1805 – £100 Vase*

Lieutenant W Carr HM Schooner Éclair
Engagement with French ship Grande Decidée off Tortola, 5 February 1804 – £50 Sword

Captain William Stanley Clarke HEIC Ship Wexford
Action of East India Company convoy against French naval squadron, Malacca Straits, 15 February 1804 – £50 Sword

Lieutenant Nicholas Brent Clements HMS Mediator
Commanding fireship during attack on French battleships, Basque Roads, 12 April 1809 – £50 Sword

Captain Cochrane HMS Kingfisher
Action off San Domingo, 6 February 1806 – £100 Vase

Captain Lord Thomas Cochrane HMS Pallas
Capture of French corvette La Tapageuse, River Gironde, 6 April 1806 – £100 Sword

Rear Admiral The Hon Sir Alexander Cochrane HMS Northumberland
Action off Saint Domingo, 6 February 1806 – £300 Vase
(*He was the uncle and godfather to Lord Thomas Cochrane above*)

Lieutenant Cole HMS Blenheim
Capture of French privateer schooner L'Harmonie, 17 November 1803 – £50 Sword

Vice Admiral Lord Collingwood HMS Royal Sovereign
Trafalgar, 21 October 1805 – £500 Vase

Lieutenant Compston HM Sloop Drake
Cutting out an American schooner from Trinité Harbour, Martinique, 19 February 1804 – £50 Sword

Captain John Conn HMS Dreadnought
Trafalgar, 21 October 1805 – £100 Sword

Mrs Cooke – widow of Captain John Cooke HMS Bellerophon Trafalgar, 21 October 1805 – £200 Vase

Lieutenant William Coombe HMS Galatea
Capture of French corvette Le Lynx, off coast of Caraccas, 21 January 1807 – £50 Sword

Lieutenant William Coote HMS Cerberus
Cutting out two vessels near St Pierre, Martinique, 2 January 1807 – £50 Sword

Lieutenant Robert Corner HMS Thisbe
Capture of the French privateer Veloce in the Mediterranean, 1 May 1804 – £50 Sword

J C Crawford HMS Pallas
Capture of the French corvette La Tapageuse, River Gironde, 6 April 1806 – £30 Sword

Lieutenant G A Crofton HMS Cambrian
Capture of the Spanish privateer schooner Maria, 13 June 1805 – £50 Sword

Captain Acheson Crozier Royal Marines HMS Centaur
Destruction of coastal battery, Martinique, 26 November 1803 – £50 Sword

Captain William Pryce Cumby HMS Bellerophon
Trafalgar, 21 October 1805 – £100 Sword

Captain James Richard Dacres HMS Bacchante
Capture of the French schooner Dauphin off Cape Raphael, 14 February 1807 – £100 Sword

Captain Nathaniel Dance HEIC Ship Earl Camden
Action between East India Company convoy and a French squadron, Malacca Straits, 15 February 1804 – £100 Sword and £100 Vase

Captain William Dawson HMS St Fiorenzo
Capture of French frigate La Piedmontese, Gulf of Manaar, 8 March 1808 – £100 Sword

Captain William Digby HMS Africa
Trafalgar, 21 October 1805 – £100 Sword

Captain William Henry Dillon HM Sloop Childers
Action with Danish warship off the Norwegian coast, 13 March 1808 – £100 Sword*

Lieutenant P J Douglas HMS Franchise
Cutting out the Spanish brig Raposa, Bay of Campeachy, 6–7 January 1806 – £50 Sword

Lieutenant Drury HMS Hydra
Attack on fort and capture of three vessels, Begu, Catalonia, 7 August 1807 – £50 Sword

Vice Admiral Sir John Duckworth HMS Superb
Action off Saint Domingo, 6 February 1806 – £400 Vase

Mrs Duff – widow of Captain George Duff HMS Mars
Trafalgar, 21 October 1805 – £100 Vase*

Captain Thomas Dundas HMS Naiad
Trafalgar, 21 October 1805 – £100 Sword

Captain R D Dunn HMS Acastra
Action off San Domingo, 6 February 1806 – £100 Vase

Captain Philip Charles Durham HMS Defiance
Trafalgar, 21 October 1805 – £100 Sword

Captain Dynely HM Packet Duke of Montrose
Capture of the French schooner L'Imperiale, 24 May 1806 – £50 Vase

Captain E Elphinstone HMS Greyhound
Destruction of the Dutch brig Christian Elizabeth, Manado, 4 July 1806 – £100 Sword

Lieutenant Matthias Everard 2nd or Queen's Royal Regiment of Foot
Capture of Monte Video, 3 February 1807 – £50 Sword

Captain Arthur Farquhar HM Bomb Ketch Acheron
Action with two French frigates, Mediterranean, 4 February 1805 – £100 Sword

Captain James Farquharson HEIC Ship Alfred
Action between an East India Company convoy and a French squadron, Malacca Straits, 15 February 1804 – £50 Sword

Captain William Ward Farrer HEIC Ship Cumberland
Action between an East India Company convoy and a French squadron, Malacca Straits, 15 February 1804 – £50 Sword*

Captain William Ferris HM Sloop Drake
Capture of the French privateer schooner L'Harmonie, 17 November 1803 – £100 Sword

Lieutenant Michael Fitton HM Schooner Pitt
Capture of the French privateer La Superbe off Cape Nicholas, 24–26 October 1806 – £50 Sword

Lieutenant John Fleming HMS Franchise
Cutting out the Spanish brig Reposa in the Bay of Campeachy, 6–7 January 1806 – £50 Sword

Lieutenant Thomas Forrest HMS Emerald
Cutting out the privateer schooner Mozambique by HM Armed Sloop Fort Diamond, Martinique, March 1804 – £50 Sword*

Lieutenant Robert Fowler, passenger on board HEIC Ship Earl Camden
Action between and East India Company convoy and a French squadron, Malacca Straits, 15 February 1804 – £50 Sword

Captain Thomas Freemantle HMS Neptune
Trafalgar, 21 October 1805 – £100 Vase

Lieutenant Thomas Furber HMS Blenheim
Capture of the French privateer schooner L'Harmonie, 17 November 1803 – £50 Sword

Lieutenant James Wallace Gabriel HMS Phoebe
Action with a French privateer, 14 July 1803 – £50 Sword

Captain The Hon Alan Gardner HMS Hero
Action off Ferrol, 4 November 1805 – £100 Sword

Lieutenant Gibson HMS Galatea
Capture of the French corvette Lynx off the coast of Caraccas, 21 January 1807 – £50 Sword

Master's Mate John Green HMS Galatea
Capture of the French corvette Lynx off the coast of Caraccas, 21 January 1807 – £30 Sword

Captain Richard Grindall HMS Prince
Trafalgar, 21 October 1805 – £100 Sword*

Captain L W Halsted HMS Namur
Action off Ferrol, 4 November 1805 – £100 Vase

Captain Archibald Hamilton HEIC Ship Bombay Castle
Action of East India Company convoy with French squadron, Malacca
Straits, 15 February 1804 – £50 Sword

Major Hammill Royal Regiment of Malta
Battle of Maida, 4 July 1807 – £100 Vase

Lieutenant J M Hanchett HMS Antelope
Capture of a Dutch Shrik, 23 March 1804 – £50 Sword

Captain George Nicholas Hardinge HM Sloop Scorpion
Capture of the Dutch ship Atalante, 31 March 1804 – £100 Sword

G Hardinge – adopted son of Captain George Nicholas HMS Fiorenzo
Capture of the French frigate La Piemontaise, Gulf of Manaar, Indian
Ocean, 8 March 1808 – £100 Vase (His stepfather was killed in this action)

Captain Thomas Masterman Hardy HMS Victory
Trafalgar, 21 October 1805 – £100 Vase

Captain William Hargood HMS Belleisle
Trafalgar, 21 October 1805 – £100 Vase

Lieutenant Haswell HMS Pallas
Capture of the French frigate La Tapageuse, River Gironde, 6 April 1806
– £50 Sword

Lieutenant George Hawkins HMS Atalante
Raiding operation in Quiberon Bay, 9 October 1803 – £50 Sword*

Midshipman George Hawkins HMS Magicienne
Capture of the Dutch vessel Schrik, 23 March 1803 – £30 Sword*

Lieutenant Robert Hayes Royal Marines HMS Hydra
Attack on a fort and capture of three vessels, Begu, Catalonia,
7 August 1807 – £50 Sword

Lieutenant Richard Head HMS Euryalus
Capture of a Danish gunboat and three smaller vessels
off the Danish coast, 11 June 1808 – £50 Sword

Surgeon John Heddle African Corps
Severe wounds received in the defence of Goree, March 1804 – £50 Vase

Lieutenant Robert Henderson HM Sloop Osprey
Capture of the French privateer La Resource, 26 October 1803
– £50 Sword

Captain William Hennah HMS Mars
Trafalgar, 21 October 1805 – £100 Vase

Midshipman James Hewitt HMS Inconstant
Cutting out a vessel under the batteries on Goree, 7 March 1804
– £30 Sword

Gunner Robert Hillier HMS Pallas
Destruction of French signal posts, summer 1806 – £30 Vase

Midshipman William Hillyar HMS Niger
Actions on 12 and 17 August 1803 – £30 Sword

Lieutenant Colonel Robert Honeyman 93rd Regiment of Foot
Capture of Cape of Good Hope, 10 January 1806 – £100 Vase

Commodore Sir Samuel Hood HMS Centaur
Action with a squadron of enemy frigates, 25 September 1806
– £300 Vase changed to two Wine Coolers*

Captain George Johnstone HMS Defence
Trafalgar, 21 October 1805 – £100 Sword

Lieutenant W J Hughes HM Fire Brig Phosporus
Action with French privateers off the Isle of Wight, 14 August 1806
– £100 Sword

Captain R G Keats HMS Superb
Action off San Domingo, 6 February 1806 – £100 Vase

Lieutenant Charles Kerr HMS Jason
Storming a fort at Aquadilla, Puerto Rico, 1 June 1806 – £50 Sword

Lieutenant King HM Sloop Drake
Storming a fort at Trinité Harbour, Martinique, 24 February 1804
– £50 Sword

Captain Richard King HMS Achilles
Trafalgar, 21 October 1805 – £100 Sword

Captain John Kirkpatrick HEIC Ship Henry Addington
Action of East India Company convoy against a French squadron,
Malacca Straits, 15 February 1804 – £50 Sword

Captain Sir Francis Laforey HMS Spartiate
Trafalgar, 21 October 1805 – £100 Sword

Lieutenant Lake HMS Blanche
Cutting out a cutter in Manchineel Bay, 5 November 1803 – £50 Sword

Midshipman Lamb HMS St Franchise
Cutting out the Spanish brig Raposa, Bay of Campeachy,
6–7 January 1806 – £30 Sword

Captain Henry Lambert HMS St Fiorenzo
Capture of the French frigate La Psyché and recapture of her prize,
Thetis off Vizagapatam, India, 14 February 1805 – £100 Sword

Boy William Langfield HM Sloop Rattler
Throwing a burning shell overboard, summer 1804 – Medal*

Captain John Richards Lapenotie`re HM Schooner Pickle
Trafalgar, 21 October 1805 – £100 Sword

Captain Thomas Larkins HEIC Ship Warren Hastings
Action of East India Company convoy against a French squadron,
Malacca Straits, 15 February 1804 – £50 Sword

Captain Sir Robert Laurie HMS Cleopatra
Action against the French frigate La Ville de Milan, 17 February 1805
– £100 Sword

Captain Thomas Lavie HMS Blanche
Capture of the French frigate La Guerriere off the Faroes, 19 July 1806
– £100 Vase

Captain James Lind HMS Centurion
Action with three French vessels while escorting a convoy in the
Vizagapatam Roads, Indian Ocean, 18 September 1804 – £100 Sword

Captain John Christopher Lockner HEIC Ship Ocean
Action of East India Company convoy with a French squadron,
Malacca Straits, 15 February 1804 – £50 Sword

Lieutenant Nicholas Lockyer HMS Tartar
Capture of the French privateer Hirondelle, San Domingo, 31 July 1804
– £50 Sword*

Rear Admiral Sir Thomas Louis HMS Canopus
Action off San Domingo, 6 February 1806 – £300 Vase

Lieutenant John Richard Lumley HMS Seahorse
Attack by boats on enemy vessels in Hieres Bay, 10 July 1804 – £50 Sword

Captain Charles Lydiard HMS Anson
Capture of Curacao, 1 January 1807 – £100 Vase

Captain Adam Mackenzie HMS Magicienne
Action off San Domingo, 6 February 1806 – £100 Vase

Lieutenant Colonel M'leod 78th Regiment of Foot
Battle of Maida, 4 July 1806 – £100 Vase

Captain The Hon Frederick Louis Maitland HMS Loire
Gallant conduct, Muros Bay, 4 June 1805 – £100 Sword

Captain Patrick Malcolm HMS Donegal
Action off San Domingo, 6 February 1806 – £100 Vase*

Lieutenant Samuel Mallock Royal Marines HMS Loire
Capture of the Spanish privateer Esperanza in the Bay of Camarinas,
2 June 1805, and the storming of the fort at Muros on 6 June 1806
– £50 Sword

Captain Charles John Moore Mansfield HMS Minotaur
Trafalgar, 21 October 1805 – £100 Sword

Boatswain John Marks HM Hired Cutter Sheerness
Protecting a captured chasse maree, 9 September 1803
– £10 Call and Chain

Lieutenant Maurice HMS Centaur
Landing on Martinique and destruction of guns, 26 November 1803
– £50 Sword

Lieutenant Giles Meech Royal Marines HMS Emerald
Attack on forts in Vivero Harbour and destruction of the French
corvette L'Apropos, 13 March 1808 – £30 Sword

Lieutenant Mends Royal Marines HMS Franchise
Cutting out the Spanish brig Raposa, Bay of Campeachy,
6–7 January 1806 – £50 Sword

Lieutenant Charles Menzies Royal Marines HMS Minerva
Storming of Fort Finisterre and cutting out five Spanish vessels,
22 June 1806 – £50 Sword

Captain Henry Meriton HEIC Ship Exeter
Action of East India Company convoy with a French squadron,
Malacca Straits, 15 February 1804 – £50 Sword

Captain William Moffat HEIC Ship Ganges
Action of East India Company convoy with the French squadron,
Malacca Straits, 15 February 1804 – £50 Sword*

Lieutenant Colonel J Moore 23rd Dragoons
Battle of Maida, 4 July 1806 – £100 Sword

Lieutenant Ogle Moore HMS Maidstone
Attack by boats on French vessels in Hieres Bay, 10 July 1804 – £50 Sword
While in HMS Minerva, cutting out five Spanish vessels, Finisterre Bay,
22 June 1806 – £50 Vase

Captain Robert Moorsom HMS Revenge
Trafalgar, 21 October 1805 – £100 Sword

Captain James Nicoll Morris HMS Colossus
Trafalgar, 21 October 1805 – £100 Vase

Captain Morrison HMS Northumberland
Action off San Domingo, 6 February 1806 – £100 Vase
(Held in trust for his son)

Lieutenant W H Mulcaster HMS Minerva
Cutting out five Spanish vessels, Finisterre Bay, 22 June 1806 – £50 Sword

Lieutenant Henry Muller HMS Tartar
Capture of the French privateer Hirondelle, San Domingo, 31 July 1804
– £50 Sword*

Captain George Mundy HMS Hydra
Attack on fort and capture of three vessels, Begu, Catalonia,
7 August 1807 – £100 Sword

Lieutenant Henry John Murton Royal Marines HMS Renommee
Cutting out the Spanish schooner Ginganta, Vieja, 4 May 1806
– £30 Sword

Mrs Nation – mother of Lieutenant Henry Walker HMS Galatea
Action against the French corvette Le Lynx off the coast of Caraccas,
in which her son was killed, 21 January 1807 – £50 Vase

Earl Nelson of Trafalgar – brother of Horatio Nelson
Trafalgar, 21 October 1805 – £500 Vase

Viscountess Nelson – widow of Horatio Nelson
Trafalgar, 21 October 1805 – £500 Vase

William Nesbitt, Master of the Berwick Smack Queen Charlotte
Gallant defence of his vessel against a French privateer, winter 1803–4
– £25 Tankard

Lieutenant Edward Nicholls Royal Marines HMS Blanche
Cutting out a cutter, Manchineel Bay, 5 November 1803 – £30 Sword
Burning a frigate, destroying a large battery in the Dardanelles, and
capture of two gunboats off Corfu (various dates) while serving
as a Captain RM in HMS Standard – £50 Sword

Rear Admiral The Earl of Northesk HMS Britannia
Trafalgar, 21 October 1805 – £300 Vase

Major Abraham Augustus Nunn
Defence of Dominica against an attempted French landing,
22 February 1805 – £50 Sword and £100 Plate

Captain Maurice Charles O'Connell 1st West India Regiment
Defence of Dominica against an attempted French landing,
22 February 1805 – £50 Sword and £100 Plate

Lieutenant James Oliver HMS Bacchante
Capture of a fort at Mariel, Cuba, 5 April 1805 – £50 Sword

Lieutenant Hyde Parker HMS Narcissus
Attack on enemy vessels by boats, Hieres Bay, 10 July 1804 – £50 Sword

Lieutenant Sir William Parker HMS Renommee
Cutting out the Spanish schooner Giganta, Vieja, 4 May 1806
– £50 Sword

Lieutenant Watkin Owen Pell HMS Mercury
Cutting out a Venetian gunboat, Rovigno Harbour, 1 April 1809
– £50 Sword

Captain Israel Pellew HMS Conqueror
Trafalgar, 21 October 1805 – £100 Sword

Captain Pelly HM Sloop Beaver
Capture of the Dutch vessel Atalante, 31 March 1804 – £100 Sword

Captain James Prendergast HEIC Ship Hope
Action involving an East India Company convoy and a French squadron,
Malacca Straits, 15 February 1804 – £50 Sword

Edward Perkyns HMS Pallas
Capture of the French corvette La Tapageuse, River Gironde, 6 April 1806
– £30 Sword

Lieutenant Charles Pickford HMS Inconstant
Whilst a prisoner, induced the French garrison of Goree
to surrender, 9 March 1804 – Vase (cost approximately £150)

Lieutenant George Pickford HMS Cambrian
Capture of the Spanish privateer schooner Maria, 13 June 1805
– £50 Sword While commanding the captured French privateer Matilda,
captured three more vessels, River St Mary's, 7 July 1805 – £100 Vase

Captain John Pilford HMS Ajax
Trafalgar, 21 October 1805 – £100 Sword

Commodore Sir Hugh Popham HMS Diadem
Capture of the Cape of Good Hope, 10 January 1806 – £200 Vase
Capture of Buenos Ayres (his flagship was now HMS Narcissus),
2 July 1806 – £200 Vase

Brigadier General George Prevost
Defence of Dominica against an attempted French landing,
22 January 1805 – £100 Sword and £200 Plate

Midshipman Priest HMS Loire
Cutting out the French brig Venteux, Isle de Bas, 27 June 1803
– £30 Sword

Captain William Prowse HMS Sirius
Trafalgar, 21 October 1805 – £100 Sword
Action off Tiber, 17 April 1806 – £100 Vase

Captain Samuel Pym HMS Atlas
Action off San Domingo, 6 February 1806 – £100 Vase

Captain Peter Rainier HMS Caroline
Action with Dutch ships, Batavia, 13 October 1806 – £100 Sword

Captain Wilson Rathbone HMS Santa Margarita
Action off Ferrol, 4 November 1805 – £100 Sword

Captain Robert Redmill HMS Polyphemus
Trafalgar, 21 October 1805 – £100 Sword

Lieutenant Robert Carthew Reynolds HMS Centaur
Capture of the French corvette Curieux, Martinique, 4 February 1804
– £50 Sword

Richard Robinson, Master of the collier Scipio
Beating off an attack by a French privateer, 26 April 1804 – £25 Tankard

Captain Edward Rotherham HMS Royal Sovereign
Trafalgar, 21 October 1805 – £100 Vase*

Lieutenant Henry Rowed Armed Cutter Sheerness
Capture of two French chasse marées, 9 September 1803 – £50 Sword

Captain William Gordon Rutherford HMS Swiftsure
Trafalgar, 21 October 1805 – £100 Sword

Mr Salmon, Master of HM Schooner L'Eclair
Cutting out the French privateer Rose, Guadaloupe, 5 March 1804
– £50 Vase

Master's Mate Barry Sarsfield HMS Galatea
Capture of the French corvette Le Lynx off the coast of Caraccas,
21 January 1807 – £30 Sword

Captain Thomas Searle HM Sloop Grasshopper
Action with French gunboats off Faro, 23 April 1808 – £100 Vase

Captain Michael Seymour HMS Amethyst
Capture of the French frigate La Thetis, 10 November 1808 – £100 Vase

Lieutenant William Shields HM Sloop Scorpion
Capture of the Dutch vessel Atalante, 31 March 1804 – £50 Sword

Captain Conway Shipley HMS Hippomenes
Capture of the French frigate L'Egyptienne, Barbados, 27 March 1804
– £100 Sword

Lieutenant Shippard (or Shephard) Armed Cutter Admiral Mitchell
Driving ashore a French brig and sloop, 31 October 1803 – £50 Sword

Lieutenant R R Sibley HMS Centaur
Attack on the French brig Le Caesar and a convoy, River Gironde,
16 July 1806 – £50 Sword

Mr Simons – father of Lieutenant Thomas Simons HMS Defiance
Trafalgar, 21 October 1805 – £100 Vase

Captain John Stewart HMS Seahorse
Capture of a Turkish vessel, Island of Scopolo, 5–6 July 1808 – £100 Vase

Rear Admiral Stirling HMS Diadem
Capture of Monte Video, 3 February 1807 – £200 Vase

Captain John Stockham HMS Thunderer
Trafalgar, 21 October 1805 – £100 Sword

Captain The Hon Robert Stopford HMS Spencer
Action off San Domingo, 6 February 1806 – £100 Vase

Rear Admiral Sir Richard Strachan HMS Caesar
Action off Ferrol, 4 November 1805 – (£300 Vase)
(The vase was never delivered and it is assumed that Strachan
received money instead)

Major General Sir John Stuart
Battle of Maida, 4 July 1806 – £300 Vase*

Mr Sutherland, Master of HMS Pallas
Capture of the French corvette La Tapageuse, River Gironde,
6 April 1806 – £50 Sword

Lieutenant Temple HMS Loire
Cutting out the French brig Venteux, Isle de Bas, 27 June 1803
– £50 Sword

Lieutenant John Thompson HMS Narcissus
Attack on enemy vessels by boats, Hieres Bay, 10 July 1804 – £50 Sword

William A Thompson HMS Pallas
Capture of the French corvette La Tapageuse, River Gironde,
6 April 1806 – £30 Sword

Captain John Fann Timins HEIC Ship Royal George
Action between an East India Company convoy and a French squadron,
Malacca Straits, 15 February 1804 – £100 Vase and £50 Sword

Captain Robert Torin HEIC Ship Coutts
Action between an East India Company convoy and a French squadron,
Malacca Straits, 15 February 1804 – £50 Sword

Mr Tracey, Secretary to Commodore Hood HMS Centaur
Capture of the French corvette Curieux, Martinique, 4 February 1804
– £30 Vase

Captain Edward Thomas Troubridge HM Sloop Harrier
Destruction of the Dutch brig Christian Elizabeth, 4 July 1806
– £100 Sword

Captain Charles Tyler HMS Tonnant
Trafalgar, 21 October 1805 – £100 Sword

Lieutenant Thomas Usher HM Armed Brig Colpoys
Capture of three Spanish luggers, Avillas, 21 March 1806 – £50 Sword

Captain Richard Budd Vincent HM Sloop Arrow
Loss of Arrow when protecting a convoy against two French frigates,
Mediterranean, 4 February 1805 – £100 Vase and £100 Sword

Lieutenant William Walker Royal Marines HMS Centaur
Landing on Martinique and destruction of coastal battery,
26 November 1803 – £30 Sword

Lieutenant Watt HMS Ville de France
Cutting out the French lugger Messager, Ushant, 17 August 1803
– £50 Sword

Lieutenant George Richard Watts HMS Comus
Cutting out the Spanish packet St Pedro, Grand Canaria, 8 May 1807
– £50 Sword

Brigade Major Weir 59th Regiment of Foot
Capture of the Cape of Good Hope, 10 January 1806 – £100 Vase

Lieutenant White HMS Beaver
Capture of the Dutch vessel Atalante, 31 March 1804 – £50 Sword

Captain Henry Wilson HEIC Ship Warley
Action between an East India Company convoy and a French squadron,
Malacca Straits, 15 February 1804 – £50 Sword

Captain William Furlong Wise HMS Mediator
Destruction of a fort at Samana, 21 February 1807 – £100 Sword

Captain James Athol Wood HMS Latona
Capture of Curacao, 1 January 1807 – £100 Vase

Captain James Wooldridge HMS Mediator
Commanding a fireship in an attack on French battleships in the
Basque Roads, 12 April 1809 – £100 Sword

Captain John Wordsworth Jnr HEIC Ship Earl of Abergavenny
Action between an East India Company convoy and a French squadron,
Malacca Straits, 15 February 1804 – £50 Sword

Lieutenant James Lucas Yeo HMS Loire
Capture of the Spanish privateer Esperanza in the Bay of
Camarinas on 2 June 1805 and storming of a fort at Muros,
4 June 1806 – £50 Vase and £50 Sword

Mrs Yescombe – widow of Captain Yescombe HM Packet King George
Gallant conduct in defence of his ship during passage from Lisbon,
31 July 1803 – £50 Vase

Lieutenant Robert Benjamin Young HM Cutter Entreprenante
Trafalgar, 21 October 1805 – £100 Sword

Captain G Younghusband HM Sloop Osprey
Attack on the French frigate L'Egyptienne, Barbados, 23 March 1804
– £100 Sword

*in the Lloyd's Nelson Collection

LLOYD'S PATRIOTIC FUND COMMITTEE 1803 AND 2003

CHAIRMEN AND SECRETARIES OF LLOYD'S PATRIOTIC FUND 1803–2003

July 1803

Sir Brook Watson
Chairman

James Abel

Sir J W Anderson

John Julius Angerstein

John Appach

George Baillie

Sir Francs Baring MP

Peter Begbie

Thomson Bonar

Thomson Bonar Jnr

George Brown

Cornelius Buller

Robert Christie

Horatio Clagett

Thomas Everett MP

John Fraser

Peter Free

Alexander Glennie

George Godwin

Benjamin Goldsmid

George Henckell

David Hunter

Germain Lavie

Richard Lee

William Macnish

John Mangles

Joseph Marryat

R H Marten

John Mavor

George Munro

Charles Offley

Thomas Raikes Jnr

Andrew Reid

Thomas Reid

Thomas Rowcroft

F S Secretan

Benjamin Shaw

James Shaw

George Shedden

Robert Shedden

John Smith MP

Henry Thompson

Robert Thornton MP

John Turner

James Warre

Thomas Warre

David Pike Watts

William Whitmore

Robert Wigram MP

George Wood

John Welsford
Secretary from 2 August

July 2003

Charles Skey TD

Anthony Asquith LVO

Clive de Rougemont

Graham Findlay

Terence Higgins

Lord Levene of Portsoken
KBE *ex-officio*

Fraser Newton

Saxon Riley

Max Taylor

Linda Harper
Secretary

Chairmen

Sir Brooke Watson, 1803

Sir Francis Baring, 1803–10

John Julius Angerstein, 1810–23

Robert Shedden, 1823–27

George Shedden, 1827–55

William Shedden, 1855–72

William Saunders, 1872–73

Sir Charles Wigram, 1873–1901

Herbert de Rougemont, 1901–15

Percy Janson, 1915–27

Charles de Rougemont, 1927–39

Sir Percy MacKinnon, 1939–55

Ernest de Rougemont CBE, 1955–77

David Beck MC, 1977–95

Charles Skey TD, 1995–

Secretaries

J P Welsford, 1803–28

J P Lines, 1828–64

J Millington, 1864–97

J Cadwallader Adams, 1898–1902

Major TD Inglis, 1903–14

Lt Col AN St Quintin OBE, 1915–27

Brig Gen WH Usher Smith CB CBE DSO, 1927–40

SW Burghes, 1941–46

GC Newby, 1946–47

Mrs LR Spicer, 1947–63

Capt GN Rawlings DSO DSC RN, 1963–68

AJ Carter, 1968–80

J Gawler, 1980–85

Mrs JH Bright, 1985–89

G Bright, 1989–92

Miss BA Lowden, 1993–94

Mrs L Harper, 1994–

Charles Skey, Chairman of the Trustees, Lloyd's Patriotic Fund.

BIBLIOGRAPHY
PRINTED SOURCES
& DOCUMENTS

Printed Sources

Dawson, Warren R. (ed.). *The Nelson Collection at Lloyd's.* London: Macmillan,1932.

Gawler, Jim. *Britons Strike Home: A History of Lloyd's Patriotic Fund, 1803-1988.* London: Pittot Publishing,1993.

Gawler, Jim. *Lloyd's Medals 1836-1989: A History of Medals Awarded by the Corporation of Lloyd's.* Toronto, Canada: Hart Publishing, 1989.

Gibb, D. E. W. *Lloyd's of London: A Study in Individualism.* London: Macmillan, 1957.

Quinton, Lt Col A. N. St OBE. *The Patriotic Fund at Lloyd's.* London: Lloyd's Patriotic Fund, 1923.

Rougemont, Herbert de. *A Century of Lloyd's Patriotic Fund, 1803-1903.* London: Leadenhall Press, 1903.

Turner, H. D. *The Cradle of the Navy: The Story of the Royal Hospital School at Greenwich and at Holbrook, 1694-1988.* The Royal Hospital School (Greenwich & Holbrook) Old Boys Association, 1990.

Wright, Charles & Fayle, C. Ernest. *A History of Lloyd's from the Founding of Lloyd's to the Present Day.* London: Macmillan, 1928.

Documents

Papers and minute book currently held by Lloyd's Patriotic Fund

Lloyd's Patriotic Fund Records deposited at the Guildhall Library, London:

Minute Books 1803-1968 (Ms31590)

Ledger 1803-1861 (Ms31591)

Domestic Letter Book 1803-1812 (Ms31592)

Foreign Letter Book 1803-1812 (Ms31593)

Foreign and Domestic Letter Books 1848-1870 (Ms31594)

Annuitants Ledger 1838-1856 (Ms31595)

South African Fund Annuitants Ledger 1905-1937 (Ms31596)

Minute Book 1969-1993 (not yet catalogued)

Annual Reports 1803-1809 (not yet catalogued)

General Correspondence files 1805-1916 (not yet catalogued)

Greenwich Hospital School Papers 1840-1928 (not yet catalogued)

Correspondence on the Royal Hospital School Greenwich under ADM 73 and 76 at the Public Record Office, Kew